SEGREGATED SKIES

DAVID HARRIS'S **TRAILBLAZING JOURNEY** TO RISE ABOVE RACIAL BARRIERS

PULITZER PRIZE–WINNING
AUTHOR

Michael H. Cottman

NATIONAL GEOGRAPHIC

WASHINGTON, D.C.

Since 1888, the National Geographic
Society has funded more than 14,000
research, conservation, education,
and storytelling projects around the
world. National Geographic Partners
distributes a portion of the funds
it receives from your purchase to
National Geographic Society to support programs including the conservation of animals and their habitats.
To learn more, visit natgeo.com/info.

For more information, visit national
geographic.com, call 1-877-873-6846,
or write to the following address:

National Geographic Partners, LLC
1145 17th Street N.W.
Washington, DC 20036-4688 U.S.A.

Representations of actual persons
(living or dead) are based on recol-
lections. In order to respect the pri-
vacy of some individuals, certain
names and physical characteristics
have been changed.

For librarians and teachers:
nationalgeographic.com/books/
librarians-and-educators

More for kids from National
Geographic: natgeokids.com

For rights or permissions inquiries,
please contact National Geographic
Books Subsidiary Rights:
bookrights@natgeo.com

Designed by James Hiscott, Jr.

Library of Congress Cataloging-in-
Publication Data

Names: Cottman, Michael H., author.
Title: Segregated skies : David Harris's
   trailblazing journey to rise above
   racial barriers / Michael H. Cottman.
Description: Washington, DC, U.S.A. :
   National Geographic Partners, [2021]
   | Includes bibliographical references
   and index. | Audience: Ages 9-12 |
   Audience: Grades 4-6
Identifiers: LCCN 2021008927 (print)
   | LCCN 2021008928 (ebook) | ISBN
   9781426371974 (hardcover) | ISBN
   9781426371981 (library binding) |
   ISBN 9781426372018 (ebook)
Subjects: LCSH: Harris, David E.,
   1934---Juvenile literature. | Air pilots--
   United States--Biography--Juvenile
   literature. | African American air
   pilots--Biography--Juvenile
   literature.
Classification: LCC TL540.H2554 C68
   2021 (print) | LCC TL540.H2554
   (ebook) | DDC 629.13092 [B]--dc23
LC record available at https://lccn.loc
   .gov/2021008927
LC ebook record available at https://
   lccn.loc.gov/2021008928

Printed in the United States
of America
21/WOR/1

A NOTE ON
LANGUAGE

The author and publisher have decided to use certain antiquated and controversial terms in the book as they were used during David Harris's lifetime. In some sections, David refers to himself, and is referred to, as a "Negro," a term commonly used from the early to mid 20th century but not used today. The word "nigger" is used in the manuscript to show the pain, torment, and effect it had in certain situations and toward particular individuals. For about 500 years, this word has been used to denigrate and demean people of African origins. In the era in which this book is set, "nigger" was used publicly and privately by non-Black people to inflict hostility, hatred, and harm and to indicate a negative perception of Black people. For many African Americans, it is the worst psychological insult. We've used it here to show what David and his family endured and to help young readers understand the embarrassment, shock, fear, and pain the word caused African American people throughout history, and, in some cases, continues to cause today.

FOR
DAVID HARRIS,
LYN MAY,
AND
LEE MAY

CONTENTS

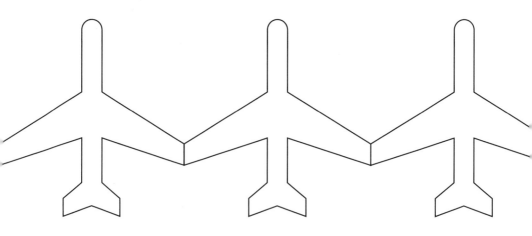

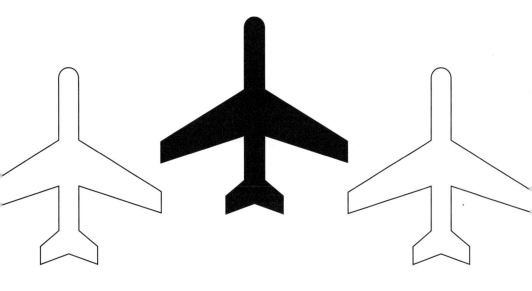

FOREWORD

✈

My name is Stephanie Hartsfield and I'm a commercial airline pilot for American Airlines, a commander in the U.S. Navy Reserve, and I'm also part of Sisters of the Skies, Inc., a nonprofit that was created to encourage and support Black women in aviation. The trailblazing pilot you're about to read about in this book is my cousin David E. Harris.

When I received the invitation to write this foreword, I was just wrapping up facilitating a class for American Airlines on "Disrupting Everyday Bias." As part of the training, participants are asked to rate a series of photos for "warmth and competence." Unbeknownst to the trainees, the last photo is actually of David, pictured in his later years in front of his own private airplane. He's wearing a warm burgundy sweater and has a soft smile on his face. Having taught this class for a couple of years now, I'm always curious to see if anyone recognizes him. I took that class myself as a trainee, and I recall blurting out excitedly, "That's my cousin!" He has changed our industry, and he is a public figure that all airline pilots should recognize.

In my family, Cousin David is a point of pride. However, it was the experience of my own discovery flight that made me realize being a pilot was something I too could love. At age 13, when I declared that I wanted to become a pilot, who did my grandparents immediately refer me to? Cousin David, of course. The first thing he did was encourage me to join the military, saying that it was one of the best ways to get trained as a pilot. He said things like, "They'll train you and you get paid to learn how to fly!" and "It's the standard for flight training in this country." I followed David's advice and eventually entered the Naval Academy to train as a pilot.

During my time there and afterward, I came to appreciate how David's legacy changed the course of my life. There was a time in the United States when Black people like us didn't have the same legal rights as white people, and wouldn't have had access to the same education, opportunities, and even basic treatment as white people. But thanks to pioneers like David, who had the courage to lead by example, break through barriers, and not take no for an answer, I can be a commercial airline pilot today—and so can you!

In keeping with the "family formula" of paying it forward, I've taken up the mantle of mentorship I've learned from Cousin David and others in my family. I've helped develop an amazing sisterhood, Sisters of the

Skies, which has been able to provide scholarships, mentorship, and the incredible experience of flight to a whole new generation of pilots. It is our hope that members of the group will create their own historic milestones in aviation history.

Throughout life, there will be people who want to hold others back while some make it their mission to lift others up. I wonder how far we could go if we all lifted each other up, if we celebrated our differences, and worked together to reach new heights.

Each of us can be a powerful example for others. My advice is to be your best self. Lift each other up. We still have so much left to achieve. Reach for the sky!

Stephanie Hartsfield,
on behalf of Sisters of the Skies

PROLOGUE
TAKEOFF

✈

David Harris grabbed his parachute and helmet, climbed into the snug cockpit of the two-seater T-37 Tweet, and took a deep breath. He was not ready to fly.

Hours earlier, David had told his instructor he needed a few more training lessons before making his first solo flight in this state-of-the-art U.S. Air Force training jet. But his instructor had been annoyed, barking at him, "You are ready!"

Now that same instructor was waving his arms in the air, pacing the tarmac, and pointing upward. "Get ready, let's go!"

David double-checked the fuel gauge and he monitored the weather the old-fashioned way: staring up at the sky. It was a clear day and all looked good. But still, he swallowed hard. A lump grew in his throat.

The flight instructor stomped closer to the airplane. His face turned bright red, his voice raspy from screaming. "We can't wait any longer! Get this bird off the ground!"

David took a deep breath. He knew by heart all the

things on the "get ready" checklist and continued to methodically go through each of them. He consulted his heading indicator, his compass, his vertical speed indicator, which measures the aircraft's rate of climb and descent, and finally his altimeter, the instrument to measure the airplane's altitude. Check. Check. Check. Everything appeared to be in working order. But was it? Should he check again? He glanced at his instructor's reddened face and knew the time was now.

David started the engines, saluted his flight instructor, locked the bubble canopy, and adjusted the throttle. The airplane taxied along the runway, faster and faster. As the landscape zoomed past and the roar of the engine filled the cockpit, David's heart raced. Gradually, he pulled back on the yoke until the wheels lifted from the ground.

The plane rose into the air.

As David looked down, tiny beads of sweat pooled on his forehead. The ground became smaller and smaller as the airplane climbed into the sky.

He glanced at his altimeter—5,000 feet, 8,000 feet, 10,000 feet.

He guided the twin-engine jet to 15,000 feet and started to laugh.

HE WAS *FLYING!*

CHAPTER 1

THRESHOLD

✈

On a hot Florida day, David Harris stepped into a crowded classroom. New to military flight school, he didn't know a soul. He nervously walked to the back of the room and selected a seat. Suddenly, he felt dozens of eyes on him.

Someone whispered, "Is he a Negro?" This wasn't the first time David had heard this, but it never got easier. Because he had light brown skin, green eyes, and light wavy hair, sometimes people misidentified him as white. David was Black and did not want to be mistaken for someone he was not. He was proud of his heritage. Occasionally, he told people his race before they asked so that strangers didn't get confused.

But sitting inside that stuffy classroom, he wasn't sure what to say, if anything. He looked around and confirmed what he had already sensed: He was the only nonwhite man among the recruits. The knot in his stomach tightened as his uneasiness grew.

David didn't want trouble. But the year was 1958 and

at that time simply being Black could mean real danger. The civil rights movement, a struggle to end segregation and empower Black people so they could have rights equal to white people, was underway. Segregation seeped into each corner of America, dividing up everything from schools to drinking fountains and even bathrooms by race.

African Americans wanted more. They wanted the same pay for jobs that white people received, the chance to buy affordable homes in desirable neighborhoods, and equality in general. But not everyone wanted this, so some people fought to keep segregation at any cost. Protests sprang up in the streets. Demonstrators marched, waving signs and placards. Tempers flared.

As this unrest unfolded, Dr. Martin Luther King, Jr., a Southern Baptist minister and a leader in the civil rights movement, preached that people should use nonviolence to bring about social change. He wanted people to fight with words and peaceful protests, instead of fists or weapons, as a way to reform the laws and overturn racist attitudes.

SIMPLY BEING **BLACK** COULD MEAN REAL DANGER.

From 1955 to 1956, Dr. King led the Montgomery bus boycott in Alabama, a protest where African Americans refused to ride city buses and the first massive demonstration against racial segregation in America. The boycott began after Rosa Parks, a Black woman, refused to give up her seat on a city bus to make room for a white passenger. Parks was arrested and charged with violating the Jim Crow laws, laws in the South that legally separated Black and white people in public places.

Black people were furious about Parks's arrest. They could not understand why the police would put her in jail simply because she refused to give up her seat to a white person.

Dr. King used his passion and words to lead the bus boycott and turn it into a national movement. He used his powerful and deep voice, full of conviction and compassion, to get people to listen. And they did. Hundreds of thousands of people traveled miles and packed churches and auditoriums to hear him speak about nonviolent solutions to these growing tensions.

At the same time that Dr. King preached about the bus boycott and urged a nonviolent response, bold newspaper headlines also tried to explain what was going on. But the media and the uproar didn't simply inform people; it also made many very uncomfortable, even afraid.

5,000 AT MEETING TO OUTLINE BOYCOTT; BULLET CLIPS BUS

NEGRO'S ARREST, $14 FINE MAY LEAD TO COURT TEST ON BUS SEGREGATION

BOTH BLACK AND WHITE CITIZENS AFFECTED BY MONTGOMERY BUS BOYCOTT

So many people lived in fear, afraid of the tension between the races, and afraid of each other. Everyone, it seemed, was trying to figure out what it meant to be Black or white and how different races could get along.

And on that first day of flight school, David wondered that himself. In the end, he decided to say nothing in response to the whispers of his classmates. He couldn't help but contemplate: What would his skin color mean for his success or failure at flight school? Or in the military? Or in his community?

And all his classmates wanted to know: Who was that green-eyed guy? Was he a Negro?

CHAPTER 2

THRUST

✈

"OPEN THOSE TEXTBOOKS, MEN!" the barrel-chested instructor

barked at the military trainees. "This is where you become aviators! Are you ready to fly and serve your country?!"

"Yes, sir!" the students shouted in unison.

"I can't hear you!" the instructor yelled while pacing the worn wooden floor.

"Yes, sir!" the students bellowed even louder. "Yes, sir!

School had been in session for a few weeks and word had started to get out that David was Black.

David heard students continue to talk about him, but not to him. He soon realized that because segregation was still so prevalent, most of his classmates had likely never spent any time interacting with an African American person before. Most of these trainees had never lived next door to a Black family or been friends with a Black kid. Most times, the other classmates' response was to pretend not to notice him, to act as if David wasn't in the room. And some of them made openly racist comments directly to him. It wasn't that they didn't know how to interact—they let him know that they didn't want to.

During the early months of flight training, David tried to be friendly. He worked hard to show his white peers the respect they would not give him. He'd glance over at a classmate and smile, only to find the trainee turn his head abruptly and look the other way. He said hello to another student in the hallway. That guy didn't respond; he kept walking. Others looked right through him. David started to feel invisible. When classes ended each day, he'd return by himself to study in his cramped room. He spent most of his time alone.

It was one thing to feel lonely, and another thing if it meant he couldn't do his job. He worried there were some white officers who would never be comfortable in the same cockpit with him while flying into battle. But that's what they were here to do, together. They were supposed to train to work as a unit, to one day possibly go to war to protect their country.

A dangerous and bloody conflict had begun in the muddy jungles of Vietnam three years earlier. David assumed one day he would fly missions overseas if the United States joined that conflict in Southeast Asia or elsewhere. And he likely would have to go to war with some of the same white men who were sitting in his flight training classroom and ignoring—or worse, hating—him.

But his anxiety about how he'd go to battle one day in the future was not nearly as urgent as his concerns about his daily life. There were problems closer to home, in Winter Haven, Florida.

Winter Haven, the town closest to the military base, is located in Polk County, a region with a long, deadly history of racism. For decades, Florida had been a stronghold for the Ku Klux Klan (KKK), a white supremacist hate group known primarily for violence toward and intimidation of Black people. Polk County was notorious for KKK mobs that marched through the dimly lit streets at night wearing their signature white robes and hoods. They'd threaten Black families by burning crosses on their lawns, and they were known for something more horrific: The KKK lynched Black people, killing them and hanging them from trees.

"I WAS SUSPICIOUS OF EVERYTHING AND EVERYONE."

In the South, more so than in the northern states, Black men were targets. They could be harassed or beaten, or even shot and killed, for no reason other than the color of their skin. David didn't want to take any chances, so he stayed on the base and kept to himself.

"I was suspicious of everything and everyone," David said. "My guard was up all the time. Nobody really had my back. There were some good people, I found out later, but it took me a while to figure out who was accepting and who may have hated me simply because I was Black."

As if the KKK wasn't enough to worry David, there was another reason he stayed on base: Emmett Till.

Emmett Till was a 14-year-old Black boy who was lynched after being accused of whistling at a white woman in a grocery store in Mississippi in 1955.

Just a year later, in 1956, as David traveled to the South on his way to Reserve Officer Training Corps (ROTC) camp, a prelude to his flight training days in the Air Force, the knowledge of what happened to Emmett was very much on his mind.

David got a ride to ROTC camp with two white cadets, other trainees. They weren't friends exactly but had agreed to drive David if he helped chip in for gas.

"I had never been South before and I may have been naive about segregation, but my mother was not," said David. "I remember she handed me a hatbox filled with fried chicken and all the trimmings: 'Honey, there won't be many places that will let you stop and eat.'"

She was right.

During the ride, David was thankful for his mother's fried chicken and her forethought. He and the other cadets were often turned away at restaurants because they didn't want to serve him. At rest stops, he sometimes wasn't allowed to use the toilet, or even to fill up the gas tank.

After David's mother's fried chicken was long gone and they were all starving, they came upon a diner. It was a shack, really. "One of the boys went into the diner to ask if they would serve me," David said. "The boy came back to the car and said I could eat in the kitchen."

David thought that was ridiculous. They'd said he could eat there, so what did it matter where he sat? He didn't want to eat in the kitchen; he wanted to eat in the restaurant. At the last minute, as he approached the diner, he decided he was going to sit in the booth with his fellow cadets. He hoped he would go unnoticed, or that maybe the restaurant owner didn't really care.

The diner was gritty, and the smell of bacon grease, fried fish, and cigarette smoke lingered in the air. Customers stared at David between their bites of hash brown potatoes and hamburgers. He wondered how many Black people had walked through the doors of the diner before him. And how had they been treated?

David tried to keep his feet from tapping nervously, fearing he would be singled out. He heard someone squeaking across the grimy floor behind him. It was the waiter who brought a plate of fried eggs and a smile to a table of white customers. But the man had harsh words for David.

"Nigger, you can eat back in the kitchen!"

David was shocked. Everyone in the diner focused their eyes on him and waited for him to make the next move. What was he supposed to do? He couldn't leave because he was riding with the other cadets. He couldn't argue with the waiter without causing major strife. He was outnumbered by impatient and seemingly hostile white patrons.

David looked at the cadets, expecting them to complain to the owner or stick up for him in some way. But there was silence. Blank stares. Indifference.

The waiter with the soiled apron and scraggily beard angrily shook his worn spatula at him. Quivering with embarrassment and some fear, David stood up and walked to the back to eat in the kitchen. As he turned away, he heard his fellow cadets order their food.

"I sat on an orange crate. My food was served on a card table that was set up in the back behind the meat counter. I didn't even eat it; I remember looking around nervously the entire time just in case someone had come to try to harm me." He thought of Emmett Till. One infraction, one offense, and the price could be your life.

"When I was ready to leave, I walked to the cash register to pay my bill and the same waiter seethed, 'Nigger, don't come up here. You go out the back door!'"

And he added, "If there's anything I hate, it's a light nigger!"

David wasn't sure how to pay for his food. Hastily, he tried to hand the waitress the money. She wouldn't touch his hand, as if she were afraid her hands would get dirty. He laid the money on the counter and left her a big tip anyway before he walked out the back door.

"As we drove off, the white customers from the diner

ONE INFRACTION, ONE OFFENSE, AND THE PRICE COULD BE YOUR LIFE.

stood at the screen door yelling at us and calling the white boys with me 'nigger lovers.'"

"For the rest of that summer at ROTC camp, I never left the base," David said.

And now, a year after he'd completed ROTC, and in another Florida city, David also stayed on base. In the evenings, instead of going out with the others, he sat alone and studied flight manuals and textbooks, hoping to excel so much in his coursework that no one could claim he didn't deserve to be there. In his free time, he read articles about the famed Tuskegee Airmen, a group of African American military fighters who earned worldwide recognition for their heroism during World War II. While this reading material wasn't required for his class, learning about the Black aviators who preceded him gave him hope that he, too, had the strength within himself to succeed. They had proven that Black pilots could be just as capable as white pilots, given the chance.

In 1941, the U.S. Army Air Corps, the forerunner of the modern-day U.S. Air Force, was segregated. Because of federal laws, Black people and white people served separately in most military divisions. During World War II, the military offered training to African Americans as pilots and mechanics. A new air base at Tuskegee, Alabama, became the center for the training program of Black aviators. These young men who aspired to become pilots encountered significant obstacles, starting with the widespread racist belief that Black people could not learn to fly or operate sophisticated airplanes.

This group quickly proved their critics wrong.

Labeled the Tuskegee Airmen, their courageous efforts earned them hundreds of medals and helped begin the eventual integration of the U.S. armed forces. The 99th Fighter Squadron, and later with the 332nd Fighter Group, flew thousands of missions in Europe and North Africa.

These men inspired David. He felt that becoming a pilot himself would somehow honor these brave airmen and preserve their legacy. The more he learned about them, the more he identified with them. "I felt close to the Tuskegee Airmen," David said. It was as if they were watching over him.

The terrifying activities of Florida's KKK, the still raw memory of the fate of Emmett Till, and the hope inspired by the Tuskegee Airmen swirled through David's mind as his flight training got underway.

With his thoughts so full of fear and promise, David wasn't sure how to interact with his fellow officers. So he grew increasingly silent and continued to spend most of his time totally alone. But he remained determined to succeed. He couldn't let his own fears or a racist society prevent him from becoming a pilot and proudly serving his country. As his training stretched into months, whenever his doubts took over, he thought of the skies, the chance to soar. Once he had experienced the thrill of that first moment of flight, that rush of adrenaline when he guided 6,000 pounds of steel into the air, he was hooked.

He had to keep flying. There was no turning back.

CHAPTER 3

FAMILY FLIGHT

✈

I t was a swelteringly hot summer day when David's best friend introduced him to Linda (Lyn) Marie Dandridge. She was smart and beautiful and had a great sense of humor. David fell deeply in love. He wanted Lyn to be a part of his life, and he wanted to start a family. On December 27, 1958, David and Lyn married.

Other significant life changes were in the works too. Being in the Air Force meant having to move frequently, sometimes with little advance notice, and David's service was no exception. Soon after his wedding, he was transferred to Webb Air Force Base in Big Spring, Texas.

Moving was always unnerving, but for this first transfer, David was ready to go. He wanted to leave Florida, where he'd felt so isolated, and start life in a new state with his new partner. He was also excited for the next phase of his career: If all went as planned, in Big Spring he would earn his wings.

In early 1959, David and Lyn arrived at Webb Air Force Base ready to make their first home together.

Because it was only a temporary assignment, they weren't allowed to live on the base. So Lyn opened the local paper, turned to the real estate listings, and started looking for apartments for rent.

At the time, Big Spring was a racially divided and hostile place for Black people. White people lived in one part of town, the nice part, and Black people lived in another section, where the housing was more dilapidated, or run-down. Being new to town, Lyn didn't really understand how segregated it was, and she certainly didn't know where the invisible borders divided the different areas. But she did know that she wanted to find a nice home for her and David—and, in particular, a place that was safe and quiet.

Thinking it might be difficult to find such a place in Big Spring, Lyn drove to another town nearby, Stanton, to explore her options. There, she spotted a FOR RENT sign posted on a private home, and she eagerly walked up the steps to the porch and knocked on the screen door.

"GET OFF MY PORCH!"

"I could see a heavyset white woman in an apron standing at a kitchen sink toward the rear of the house, her back to the door," Lyn recalled. "She turned and looked at me for a very long minute. It was not a friendly look. I told her I was there about the room to rent."

Then the woman started screaming, "Get off my porch!"

LYN WASN'T **SUPPOSED** TO BE IN **THAT** PART OF TOWN; IT WAS FOR **WHITES** ONLY.

Lyn recalled, "I was so stunned, I stayed rooted to the spot. When I didn't move she raised her voice and said, 'Nigger, get off my damn porch!'"

"I left as fast as I could," Lyn said.

Lyn wasn't supposed to be in that part of town; it was for whites only. A local Black resident would have known to stay away from that obviously white neighborhood, and not walk up to a white stranger's porch to ask to rent a room.

"I literally didn't know any better," Lyn said. "I was desperate to find us a place to live, and I was 18 years old and it simply didn't occur to me to think I was breaking a social, and perhaps actual, law." She was shaken but had to get back out there to continue her search.

Days later, running out of options, she found a place on a side of town that was for Blacks only. She and David had a hard time feeling happy about the accommodations, however. The small wooden structure was nothing more than a hovel on the side of a dried-up riverbed. It had three rooms, placed one after another. Standing at the front door, a person could look straight through and out the back door.

They did their best to settle in, but the sacrifice of moving to the segregated neighborhood did not mean they escaped bigotry. Lyn and David had to shop and buy gas in town, which meant that even if they tried to keep their heads down and avoid trouble, trouble sometimes found them.

One incident in particular stands out in Lyn's memory. Months after their move, as she walked along a sidewalk in downtown Big Spring in a brand-new white skirt, she encountered a group of men sitting on a bench outside a hardware store. The men watched her intently, and she became afraid. She stared straight ahead and hurried to get past them. "I heard that hawking noise of someone gathering phlegm in the back of their throat. His aim was good. He left a long, gross tobacco stain down the back of my white skirt," she later recounted.

Lyn hurried home, fighting back tears. Once there, she ripped off the skirt—now ruined—and changed clothes. Outside, she put the skirt in an old empty oil can and set it on fire. She watched it burn into curled, brown fragments.

At that moment, to Lyn, it wasn't just about losing an expensive piece of her wardrobe. She felt violated. These men had spat their anger and hatred onto her and made her feel powerless to stop them. As that skirt turned to ash, so too did some of her faith in her place in America.

When David came home later that evening, she didn't say a word about it. She wanted the whole incident to go away, to burn up like the skirt itself. She felt an illogical sense of shame. As if she had somehow done something to invite this treatment, and for not standing up for herself. But what could she have done? If she had yelled, screamed, made a scene, would she be attacked? She was also afraid for David. She loved him very much and wanted to keep him safe. She couldn't take any chances that he would become angry and try to confront these men. And so, she kept her secret.

As David and Lyn continued to walk through the insults and threats in this segregated Texas city, David worked hard on his demanding flight training.

With Lyn by his side, David focused on being a good airman and preparing to fight for his country. He continued to put his all into school. Finally, in July of 1959, his work and efforts paid off, and he graduated. Inside the classroom on that last day, David's flight training instructor handed him a small wing-shaped badge.

There was no graduation celebration. No music or dancing, no hoopla with the other officers, no tossing of tassel caps in the air, and no speeches.

That night, David and Lyn sat in the silence of their tiny, unair-conditioned apartment, and David breathed with relief. He'd persevered in a system where the odds were against him. The two hugged each other tightly and stared at the small wings pinned to his lapel.

David was now a U.S. Air Force pilot.

For his first assignment, David would be sent for advanced training at McConnell Air Force Base in Wichita, Kansas, where he'd become certified to fly B-47s. But first he had to complete a mandatory two-week survival course in the Nevada desert.

For the survival course, David was required to camp in the wilderness for a week with a military unit, far from any city, and find his own food. David understood that this training was important. If he was ever at war and abandoned in enemy territory or had to eject from a distressed plane, the lessons he learned here could one day save his life. This exercise would only be a simulation, but it felt real, and he knew the test would be daunting. He'd heard that not all of the recruits made it through successfully. No matter how hungry or tired he became, David knew one thing for sure: He was not going to give up.

"After an orientation in the classroom, they put us in a truck and dropped us in the wilderness with nothing but a canteen of water and a small survival kit containing only a few nutritional bars," David recalled. "They told us to live off the land."

David's commander gave him a piece of a parachute and a string to replicate what he would have left after bailing out of an airplane in war. Not much to work with. It was hard to find things to eat. Of his experience, David said, "One day, because I was so hungry, I ate a black ant!"

By the time David returned to his base camp, he was completely exhausted, thirsty, and covered in dirt stains. But he'd survived and was filled with a sense of accomplishment and pride.

He knew there would be more challenges, more situations where he'd need to worry about his survival. But for now, he was proud of his wings, proud to call himself a U.S. Air Force pilot, and ready for what lay ahead.

CHAPTER 4

CLEARANCE

✈

The ear-piercing screech of the military alarm shook David from a nervous sleep.

"Go! Go! Go!" a commander yelled inside the Air Force barracks. "Move! Move! Move!"

With David's flight training over, he landed an assignment at Plattsburgh Air Force Base in New York. He and Lyn moved there in the spring of 1960 and soon welcomed their first child, Camian (Cami) Lee Harris, a baby girl.

David was now a B-47 co-pilot and a dad.

That year was full of sleepless nights. It wasn't just cries from their newborn that kept David awake: He had to always be prepared for war, ready to be called on to fly into combat in the middle of the night. Every few weeks, he left home to spend days "on alert" at the base. There, he slept in a barrack with his squadron and spent his nights and days ready to spring into action. It was a jittery existence and David often felt on edge.

At the time, the United States was facing increased

pressure on multiple fronts. It was in the midst of the Cold War, a long period of tension between the United States and the communist countries of Eastern Europe led by the Soviet Union, some of which is now called Russia. And while the United States hadn't officially entered the Vietnam War, the number of U.S. military personnel in the region was growing exponentially. It seemed any minute U.S. involvement would become official.

It was during one of his "on alert" nights at the base when the military alarm went off. David quickly grabbed his helmet and parachute. His flight uniform was wrinkled from tossing and turning in his bunk, but that didn't matter now.

He ran in step with his crew as fast as he could across the dark tarmac to the huge B-47 bomber. Under the blare of the alarm and commanders' shouts, they scrambled up the ladder into the tight cockpit, closed the bubble canopy, and strapped themselves into the navigator and pilot seats. They cranked up all six turbojet engines and were ready to take off. But they had no idea where they were going or what their assignment was.

As David waited for further instruction, his heart pounded. His brain, still groggy from sleep, tried to catch up. This could be a drill. But if it was the real thing and he was being sent on a mission, he could face any number of dangers, from being shot down in enemy territory to missiles being launched at him. Where was he going? Would he be commanded to drop bombs? What would be the target? Would he make it home? What was the last thing he said to Lyn? He couldn't remember ...

Shaking himself out of that line of thought, he forced his mind to relax and instead leaned on his training to keep his movements steady. He had to fly, that was all. He'd done it a hundred times. He was good at it. He could do this.

Through his headset, he heard the commander's voice. It was a coded message that David was required to decipher within seconds. Only then would he know what his mission was, or if this was just a drill. His stomach clenched as he focused. Then ... he got it.

It was just a drill.

He exhaled in relief.

But he couldn't go back to bed—not just yet. As part of the training, he was still required to take off as if he was going on a mission.

As the thud of his heartbeat in his ears faded away, replaced by the deafening roar of the engine, David adjusted the throttle and raced down the runway. Within seconds, he pulled back the yoke and, with rocket assist on takeoff, felt the rush of the B-47 and all of its 204,000 pounds slowly lift into the sky, airborne.

Although David didn't fly into battle that night, he was soon sent away on assignment. As the strained relationship between the Soviet Union and the United States intensified, the number of U.S. military personnel increased at international bases to prepare for a battle between the two superpowers. The two countries were in an arms race to amass nuclear bombs—destructive weapons with the power to destroy whole cities. In the United States, fear of nuclear impact prompted ordinary people to build bomb shelters and teachers to drill their students in how to take cover during a nuclear attack. Movies, comics, and books featured postapocalyptic landscapes and mutant creatures, all caused by these terrible bombs.

It seemed as if fear was everywhere when David was sent on a temporary tour of duty at Brize Norton Airfield in England, about two hours from London. From there, U.S. forces closely monitored the movements of the Soviet Union. David was assigned to the nuclear-armed B-47 bombers for the Strategic Air Command.

At the base, U.S. commanders assembled pilots and crews for frequent drills. When the high-pitched alarm sounded, everyone scrambled into action. Now, hearing the alarm, David remained calm. He'd grown more accustomed to dealing with these late-night sirens.

The B-47, a six-engine, turbojet-powered strategic bomber, used state-of-the-art nuclear technology and flew at supersonic speed. It could fly 600 miles an hour at extraordinarily high altitudes to avoid enemy intercep-tor aircraft. This multimillion-dollar aircraft was capable of carrying the most powerful weapons. It was also equipped with three ejection seats, so David and the two other crewmen could bail out if there was a mechanical problem or if the airplane was hit by enemy fire. In addition to flying the airplane at high altitudes, David also had to be ready to jump out of it.

Each B-47 had a three-man crew. The military required the crew to stay together at all times. They had to be on alert 24 hours a day in case they were ordered into war.

"We ate together, went to the barbershop together, studied together, and even went to the bathroom together!" David recalled, laughing.

David's crew came from different parts of the States and different backgrounds in general, and it was hard to imagine where these three men would have met if they hadn't been thrown together. But they grew close, as officers and friends. They relied on one another for their survival, not just training for

DAVID FINALLY FELT LIKE HE FIT IN.

war but for the tiny movements and practical details of everyday life. Again, David was different: He was the only Black pilot in his unit, the only Black man in this tight-knit group of aviators who spent all their time together. But they established relationships built on trust. And despite his skin being a different color, because of their personalities and the fact that they were stuck together, David finally felt like he fit in. He was just one of the guys, a pilot waiting for orders like everyone else.

But David wouldn't stay with the same crew forever. He was about to move again.

In June 1962, David and Lyn relocated to another temporary assignment at Castle Air Force Base in Merced, California, where he upgraded to the massive B-52. The B-52, with its eight engines, could weigh up to 480,000 pounds and was capable of carrying 70,000 pounds of weapons, including nuclear bombs. With six crew members, the B-52 could fly 650 miles an hour with a range of 12,000 miles. Valued at some $14 million, it was the largest, most powerful, and most expensive airplane in the world at the time. And David was about to fly it.

But being entrusted by the Air Force to handle one of the world's most costly and formidable machines didn't mean he had freedom on the ground. Racial segregation continued, even in Merced. David and Lyn were forced again to live in a segregated neighborhood in the Black and Hispanic part of town. They rented another narrow, small dwelling with rooms arranged one behind the other. It wasn't much, but it was a house they could afford in the only part of town where they could legally live. They spent a long, dry, hot summer in central California.

Then later that year, in August 1962, David was reassigned to Westover Air Force Base in Chicopee, Massachusetts, where as a B-52 co-pilot, he rose to the rank of captain. David and his family settled into another house, off base at first until base housing became available. And while the family went about their lives, adjusting to yet another home, another move, and another community, David faced a military emergency.

CHAPTER 5

READY FOR WAR

avid climbed into the cockpit of the B-52 bomber, strapped himself into the cramped seat, started all eight engines on the dark tarmac, and consulted with his crew. Then he did something that made him uncomfortable: He waited.

For 13 days in October 1962, the world watched nervously as the United States stood on the brink of nuclear war during the Cuban Missile Crisis. During this direct and dangerous confrontation between the United States and the Soviet Union, leaders of the two countries engaged in a political and military standoff. The Soviet Union wanted to install missiles on Cuba, just 90 miles from U.S. shores. After 15 years of simmering tensions of the Cold War, it was the moment when the two superpowers came closest to nuclear war.

In a TV address on October 22, 1962, President John F. Kennedy notified Americans about the presence of the missiles, explained his decision to put up a naval blockade around Cuba, and made it clear the U.S. was prepared to use military force if necessary to stop Soviet missiles from being installed.

And at Westover Air Force Base, David was told to prepare to drop bombs somewhere, maybe even Cuba. His mission was top secret.

Sure enough, one night he was ordered to his plane, where he had to sit still and wait in a machine likely equipped with nuclear missiles.

"I hadn't been trained on the B-52 very long, but if the Air Force had to drop bombs, I knew I would be a part of it. I'd be right in the middle of it," David recalled.

"While I knew my plane could hold different types of weapons, I didn't know what type they'd loaded onto the plane and if we would be ordered to drop nuclear weapons. We were on high alert and there was a lot of anxiety. I thought about my family—about my daughter, Cami, and about Lyn, who was pregnant. We were expecting another baby."

For the first time, David thought he might not survive this mission. His service to his country could cost him his life. He loved his family and wanted to be there when his next child was born. Inside that musty cockpit with a faint smell of jet fuel, he thought about his duty to his country and his duty to his family.

How could he best protect his family? He wished he had a photograph of them to look at, but he couldn't bring anything personal in the airplane. If he crash-landed in enemy territory, he wasn't supposed to have any infor-mation that the enemy could use against him. He thought about this as he and his flight crew waited for orders, all the while keeping his hand gripped on the throttle and listening to the roar of the massive jet engines.

"When I made a decision to serve my country," David recalled, "I didn't have a family. And then just a few years later, there I was on duty to drop bombs and now I had a family that, at that moment, I couldn't even call. I wouldn't even have a chance to say goodbye to the people I loved."

Thankfully, that day, disaster was avoided. The United States agreed to the Soviet leader's offer to remove the missiles in exchange for the United States promising not to invade Cuba. With the crisis over, David was asked to steer the huge airplane back to the hangar. He climbed out of the cockpit, relieved to have avoided going to war and sure disaster.

HIS SERVICE TO HIS COUNTRY COULD COST HIM HIS LIFE.

But to David, it felt as though there was turmoil everywhere. Even though nuclear war had been averted, another battle raged at home on U.S. soil. Just weeks before the Cuban Missile Crisis, James Meredith, a civil rights activist, became the first Black student to enroll at the segregated University of Mississippi. President Kennedy sent 5,000 federal troops to contain the rioting that resulted from Meredith's enrollment. Then on November 20, Kennedy signed an executive order banning segregation in federally funded housing. The order prohibited discrimination in the sale, leasing, or rental of properties and facilities owned or operated by the federal government.

At the same time, in Mississippi, a Black woman named Fannie Lou Hamer encouraged thousands of African Americans to become registered voters. She also worked to help hundreds of poor people through her programs like the Freedom Farm Cooperative. As she worked, Hamer was threatened, harassed, shot at, and assaulted by individuals who didn't want Black people to vote.

Between this constant civil unrest and the dangers he could face at any moment resulting from the Cold War, David's life filled with stress. Above everything else, he wanted to provide a stable home and future for his family. But after the Cuban Missile Crisis, David wasn't sure the military was the right path for him. What if he were killed in battle and left his family without a father and husband?

On August 5, 1963, David and Lyn welcomed their second daughter, Leslie Carol Harris. The thought of a future of frequently moving from one Air Force base to another, uprooting their children from their schools and friends, and being on 24-hour call to drop bombs any-where in the world on a moment's notice was really wearing on him. David was concerned about all the middle-of-the-night exercises and war preparations. Uneasy about not being there to help his wife raise their children, he agonized more and more about the dangers of hauling nuclear bombs and listening to the earsplitting sound of the military alarm.

The prospect of his squadron being sent to Vietnam also became a greater possibility, and he began to question the rightness of that mission. He started to think about other career possibilities. At the time, the commercial airline industry was expanding rapidly, offering jobs to former military pilots.

Would a more stable, "normal" lifestyle be best for Lyn and his two young daughters? If he continued with the military, would he be around to see his girls take their first steps, graduate from high school, attend their proms? Was that the life David wanted for his future? For his family?

Making the decision to leave the military was not easy. David felt it was an honor to serve his country, and he wondered if he would be hired to work anywhere else. After all, there were no African American commercial airline pilots in the United States. Not yet. But flying was what David knew. It was what he had worked for his whole life. How could he let that go?

After many sleepless nights, looking at all sides of the argument, David concluded that he had to make a change.

CHAPTER 6

CROSSWINDS

✈

David had decided to leave the military. But first, he'd need a job. He grew excited by the prospect of flying for a major commercial airline. But in the evenings after the kids fell asleep, he'd confide to Lyn that he was anxious, too, about what the future could hold. Even as he second-guessed his decision to leave the Air Force, he updated his résumé and tried to set up interviews. He sent letters seeking employment to several different airlines. He ensured his writing was flawless, with no misspelled words, impeccable grammar, and a strong argument for why they should hire him.

As he started his job search, Black people across the United States continued to fight for equal opportunities in the workforce and elsewhere. Volatile racial unrest accompanied the fight. The nation's memories were still fresh from the massive 1963 March on Washington, which took place three months earlier and where an estimated 300,000 people gathered at the Lincoln

Memorial in Washington, D.C., to listen to Dr. King deliver his legendary "I Have a Dream" speech.

It was the largest gathering for civil rights of its time. People from all over the country arrived in the nation's capital by planes, trains, cars, and buses. With so many gathered to protest this heated issue, President Kennedy grew concerned that there could be violence and asked for support to keep the city safe. The Washington, D.C., police force mobilized nearly 6,000 officers, and the federal government assigned 6,000 soldiers and National Guardsmen for additional protection.

In the end, the crowds were calm and peaceful, and there were no incidents reported by the police.

That day, Dr. King stood before the crowd and said, "I have a dream that my four little children will one day live in a nation where they will not be judged by the color of their skin, but by the content of their character."

Those words resonated with David. Like Dr. King, David treasured fatherhood. He hoped his young Black children could grow up without having to experience racism. And just as Dr. King preached that we should be judged on our merits, David too wanted to land a job with a major commercial airline because of his skills, and not be rejected simply because of the color of his skin.

The March on Washington was also called the March on Washington for Jobs and Freedom. This name spoke directly to the inequalities that David now faced head-on in his own career.

David wasn't naive about the discrimination a Black

person potentially faced in the job market. He knew that he was extremely qualified, so on paper he would seem like an ideal candidate to many commercial airlines. But once he was brought in for an interview, and a prospective employer saw the color of his skin, he was concerned that he would face disappointment again and again. He could be yelled at, thrown out of the office, or chastised for "duping" people. He also feared that if employers discovered he was Black after he was hired, he might be fired anyway. He decided it would be best for him to be up front about who he was and head off any potential conflict. He wanted to find an airline that would bring him in anyway, someone willing to take a chance on him.

And so, he ended his application letter with this simple statement: "I'm married, I have two children, and I'm a Negro."

He sent his letters off and, one by one, the rejections came in. One airline didn't respond to his application. Another refused to give him an application when he showed up in person. Another airline claimed he failed a test that David knew he had aced.

Finally, he received an offer for an interview. The stakes were high; this was his last and only chance. David reconsidered his decision to be forthright about his race. After all, he was light-skinned enough to pass for being white. Perhaps the interviewer hadn't seen his application and didn't know his race. When he walked into that interview, would he dare to remind the hiring pilot that he was Black?

CHAPTER 7

CHANGING COURSE

David waited in the cavernous lobby for his interview with American Airlines—the only interview offer he'd received after sending out a number of letters and résumés.

Sitting in that reception area, he was acutely aware of his skin color, which contrasted with the paler skin tones of the professionals seated around him. He thought about how there were no African American commercial airline pilots anywhere in the United States. If he were hired, he'd be the first. It wasn't a comforting thought. The likelihood of this interview ending in rejection seemed high.

After all, even the Tuskegee Airmen, American heroes, his personal heroes, had been shunned by the commercial airline industry. From the countless articles he'd read about them, David had become somewhat of an authority on their legacy. After completing their training at Tuskegee, Alabama, on July 19, 1941, some of the airmen were sent to North Africa. There they were assigned secondhand P-40 airplanes that were tough and durable but slow and obsolete, unable to maneuver as easily as the German Messerschmitt Bf 109 or the Focke-Wulf FW 190 fighters they faced.

By the summer of 1944, these Black pilots, having shown great skill, had earned more of the military's trust and were given P-51 Mustangs, which were much faster and more sophisticated. They used these for their primary missions, escorting bombers striking targets in southern Europe. For easy recognition in the skies, the group painted their aircraft's tails in a distinctive red, which led to their legendary nickname, the "Red Tails."

Among the pilots who had shown tremendous grit and perseverance was Daniel "Chappie" James, Jr., the first African American to reach the rank of four-star general in the U.S. Air Force. James had overcome tremendous racial bias to lead battle operations overseas. He fought in both the Korean War and the Vietnam War, flying more than 160 combat missions and leading the Bolo MiG sweep of 21 communist aircraft.

Benjamin O. Davis, Jr., the son of an Army general and a 1936 graduate of West Point, led the 99th Fighter Squadron, the Army Air Corps' first all-Black air unit. Davis went on to lead the 332nd Fighter Group in Europe during World War II. Later, he earned the rank of lieutenant general and played a critical role during the Korean and Vietnam Wars.

Franklin Macon, an original Tuskegee Airman, studied aeronautics and learned to fly through the Civil Air

Patrol in high school. Racism wasn't the only obstacle he'd faced: He overcame issues with dyslexia, a condition that made it difficult for him to read, to become a fighter pilot. Macon survived dozens of dangerous missions and served with distinction during World War II.

Thinking of these pilots gave David a kernel of optimism. They'd come so far, and now it was his turn to take their progress a step further. He didn't have any mentors in his

field, only these men. *Heroes.* He turned the word over and over in his mind as he waited nervously for his interview to begin.

David knew he was qualified. He was a good pilot. He could do the job and do it well. He believed in himself. And now it was time for him to believe in others, that they were good and would do the right thing. That this interviewer would give him an honest, unbiased opportunity. After all, his application stated that he was Black and he was still brought in. And that was reassuring, wasn't it?

"Mr. Harris," the interviewer's secretary said to David, "time for your interview. Please follow me."

CHAPTER 8

FLIGHT PLAN

✈

David stood up quickly, ready for action, eager to get to the interview. Gathering his notes, he followed the secretary into a small, stuffy office at JFK International Airport, where she asked him to take a seat and wait again.

David took the chance to review his handwritten notations on the job application. He rehearsed responses to possible interview questions, thinking about how he could best present his aviation skills.

In the back of his mind, David knew this airline was his best, and possibly only, option. But he also knew that he couldn't let desperation drive this interview. A pilot needs to be calm, collected, self-assured—ready and able to command a giant, complicated aircraft and up to the task of ensuring the safety of the passengers on board. David took a deep breath and tapped into his years of military training to calm his racing mind and focus on the task at hand, rather than on the what-ifs.

It seemed like hours had passed, but it was probably

only a few minutes, before a heavyset white man with a sunburned face walked into the tiny office and took a seat in a tall swivel chair behind a large desk. The man introduced himself as the chief pilot for American Airlines.

The man leaned back in his chair and plopped both his feet on top of his desk. His tone came across as informal as his posture when he started to speak, all the while peering through his hard-sole shoes.

David's heart sank as he witnessed his interviewer's casual approach. This meeting was vitally important to David's life, but it seemed like the chief pilot, with his feet on the desk, didn't care. David's calm cracked a little as he wondered if the man had come in there with his decision already made. Had he read the closing sentence of David's letter?

David swallowed and felt a lump grow in his throat. He fought a feeling of hopelessness. Would anything he say matter at this point? But he thought of his family, and he thought of flying. And that gave him strength. He was an expert on all things aviation. He deserved to be here. He had completed so many trainings and flown countless missions. What little free time he had, he spent reading about other pilots, other flight stories. Flying was what he knew. And he knew it well. His mood shifted and he suddenly felt animated—good, in fact— and ready for questions.

"Why do you want to be a pilot?" the chief pilot asked in a booming voice. It was the kind of voice that could be intimidating, even aggressive.

He considered responding by citing his aviation skills. He could talk about his deep knowledge of math and physics, his ability to make quick intelligent decisions in the cockpit, his leadership potential, and his propensity to remain composed in a crisis.

But as David looked back at his interviewer, he decided to answer simply and with conviction, "I'm a good pilot. And I want to fly."

And then David uttered a few provocative words he hoped he would not regret. "I don't want there to be any misunderstandings with you or your company," David told the chief pilot. "I am a Negro. I'm a little concerned because I've put this in a lot of applications at other airlines and I was turned down."

WHAT MORE COULD HE DO TO PROVE HIMSELF?

A thick silence enveloped the room. The chief pilot sat up straight in his chair and stared at David intensely from behind his desk, as though to verify for himself.

As David and the chief pilot looked at each other from across the desk, David wondered what the other man saw. Was it his Blackness? Or did he look at David and see a captain in the U.S. Air Force, someone strong and capable? What more could he do to prove himself?

The chief pilot continued to stare at David and began to tap his pencil on the desk. "Young pilot," he finally said, "this is American Airlines. We don't care if you're Black, white, or chartreuse. We only want to know this: Can you fly the plane the right way?"

David was so stunned and excited by the chief pilot's words that they took a moment to register. "Yes, I can!" he responded enthusiastically.

The chief pilot was not very long-winded. After a few more questions, he told David that he would review his application and someone from American Airlines would be in touch.

David exhaled and shook the chief pilot's hand.

"Thank you for coming in," the chief pilot said in a noncommittal voice. "Have a nice day."

CHAPTER 9

FULL
THROTTLE

✈

Weeks passed after David's interview with American Airlines. In the meantime, he continued to work at Westover Air Force Base, but his days with the military would soon end.

On the morning of November 30, 1964, while David was working on the base, he received a telegram.

Telegrams carried important, personal news back then, and David didn't know what to expect. Had something terrible or wonderful occurred? Was it a family emergency? He took a deep breath, paused for a moment, and walked to a quiet corner of the room, away from the other men. He unfolded the bright yellow telegram slowly and read the first four words that appeared in large type. And then he reread them, not believing what he saw.

"WELCOME TO AMERICAN AIRLINES!"

It was a short telegram with only a few lines. It told David to report to Dallas, Texas, within the week and listed the person to contact once he arrived.

David wanted to shout for joy, but he was, after all, a captain in the U.S. Air Force, which meant he needed to continue to be a model of composure and a poised leader. So he didn't tell any of the officers working around him. Instead, he walked outside, broke into a broad smile, and allowed himself one exuberant fist pump in the air. He couldn't wait to share his good news with Lyn!

David was thrilled, but he knew this didn't mean everything would be OK. Getting the job was one thing, keeping the job, and excelling as the nation's first Black pilot hired by a commercial passenger airline, would be something altogether different. The Civil Rights Act had passed only five months before, and while David knew the law meant employers weren't supposed to discriminate in hiring people based on the color of their skin, he questioned how long it would take for many companies to actually follow the law. Or if they would continue to discriminate in other ways once the employee was hired.

While the Civil Rights Act was a long time coming, the months leading up to it were particularly weighty. Nearly a year before its passage, members of the Ku Klux Klan planted a bomb at the 16th Street Baptist Church in Birmingham, Alabama, killing four young African American girls during church services. More than a dozen others were also injured in the explosion. Three KKK members would be convicted of murder in connection with the bombing years later, but in the immediate aftermath, Black residents took to the streets to mourn their loss and also to riot in anger. The riots led to violence, and Governor George Wallace sent 500 National Guardsmen and 300 state troopers to the city to quell the upheaval.

President Kennedy responded by saying, "If these cruel and tragic events can only awaken that city and state—if they can only awaken this entire nation to a realization of the folly of racial injustice and hatred and violence—then it is not too late for all concerned to unite in steps toward peaceful progress before more lives are lost."

President Kennedy had proposed the Civil Rights Act, and it had been met with strong opposition in Congress. But then, tragically, he was assassinated in November 1963 and Lyndon B. Johnson, the vice president, became president of the United States. Johnson supported the act and made an emotional appeal to Congress.

"No memorial oration or eulogy could more elo-quently honor President Kennedy's memory than the earliest possible passage of the civil rights bill for which he fought so long," Johnson told legislators in his first address to Congress. "Let this session of Congress be known as the session which did more for civil rights than the last hundred sessions combined."

Congress finally agreed and Johnson signed the

historic Civil Rights Act in July 1964. The act formally ended segregation in public places and banned employment discrimination on the basis of race, color, religion, sex, or national origin.

Many Americans celebrated, but unfortunately the law was not always followed, and it was hard to enforce. Some states and people still abided by Jim Crow laws, and there was the emergence of angry vigilantes, people who enforced segregation illegally. The Civil Rights Act was a great advancement, but there was still a lot to do before it would be put into practice, and truly accepted, across the country.

During this time, Dr. King continued to preach for equality, and his work helped sway public opinion. The same year, Dr. King was awarded the Nobel Peace Prize for his powerful leadership that helped bring about racial equality through nonviolence. At 35 years old, Dr. King became the youngest person to receive the award to date.

And now, at age 30, Captain David Harris prepared to walk through one of the doors that Dr. King and President Johnson had opened for him. From the Birmingham bombing to the Civil Rights Act, from white vigilantes to Dr. King's Nobel Peace Prize, David knew progress was being made even as racist events continued to unfold. As he prepared to accept this new job, the pressure on him was immense. He could not afford to make any mistakes.

How would he manage any racial problems if they

came up at work? What if he encountered white pilots who didn't want to fly with him because he was Black? Could individuals overcome long-standing and deep-rooted personal prejudices? Could his new employer? David knew he'd be watched more closely than ever, and he wanted to be successful, for himself and his own career, but also because he had to set the path for other Black pilots who would come after him.

The stakes were particularly high. On the one hand, David was thrilled and ready to take the job; on the other hand, he still felt tense and nervous. Before he officially accepted the position, he questioned his decision yet again.

A few days after receiving the telegram, David and Lyn set out to run errands, both preoccupied, as they thought about their uncertain future. Instead of talking, they rode in silence. Sure, American Airlines knew his race, but David wondered if there was some unforeseen hitch it hadn't considered. What if the airline changed its mind and decided it wasn't interested in being part of history after all? What if it reversed its hiring decision? What if it didn't want David to succeed? What if it wanted to use him as an example of why Black people shouldn't or couldn't fly commercial jets? Was he being set up for failure?

As they approached the base's main gate, instead of turning in to head home, David kept driving around the traffic circle before the main gate. Lyn glanced at him. "Where are you going?" she asked.

"What should I do?" David asked, his eyes on the road. Lyn, who was never without an opinion, was uncharacteristically silent. He looked over at her as he continued to drive. Everything—the air, the car, his mind—felt heavy, as though life were happening in slow motion.

"Do what you want to do. What your heart tells you to do. We're with you no matter what you decide," Lyn said.

Once she'd gotten the words out, Lyn's unease lifted. This had to be David's decision alone. He'd be the one in the spotlight, facing whatever difficulties that came with taking such a huge risk.

David sank deeper into thought, finally turning back to the base, returning the salute at the guardhouse and driving the short distance to their house. Lyn thought he seemed angry, but she remained silent. She'd said all she had to say.

Inside the house, they went their separate ways, Lyn putting away groceries while David walked to another room. Soon David returned to the kitchen and stood beside Lyn. "I'm doing it," he said. "I'm going to take the job with American."

It was done. Quietly, in two simple sentences, their lives changed. David submitted his notice to be released from duty; he was leaving the military to become a civilian.

David took his new job very seriously, including the initial step, which was to report to training at company headquarters. Sure, he knew how to fly, but commercial airplanes were not bomber jets. He had to learn this company's particular rules and regulations. These airplanes were somewhat smaller than the massive B-52 bombers. He'd now carry a plane full of civilians instead of airmen, food and beverages instead of military gear, and suitcases instead of weapons.

From the first moment he was hired, he was "a Black man in the very act of proving he was as good at his job as a white man," Lyn said. "Learning new things in a new environment was secondary to carrying the hopes of every Black man on his shoulders. David had the steady focus, courage, and willingness to put himself out there and risk failure. To risk having no job at all," she said.

As David packed his bag and prepared to leave for training, he knew he owed thanks to Marlon Green, a man who also fought for the advancement of Black aviators. David was aware he would not have been hired without the persistence of this great pilot.

In the late 1950s, Green, a Black military pilot, sued Continental Airlines for racial discrimination after they refused to hire him despite his stellar military record. At his own personal expense, Green waged a six-and-a-half-year court battle with Continental. The airline argued that racist white passengers would refuse to fly with a Black pilot and that Continental would not be able to find hotels for Green during layovers in the southern United States, where segregation laws were still enforced. But in a landmark U.S. Supreme Court decision in 1963, Continental was ordered to hire Green. David knew that without that ruling, he might never have been hired. As it turned out, David secured a job first, and Green, hired subsequently, went on to fly from 1965 to 1978.

"Marlon Green," David said, "is part of aviation and civil rights history. He paved the way for me and for many other Black pilots who followed."

The Civil Rights Act, the civil rights movement, and the Supreme Court decision supporting Green all helped David get the job he wanted, but they did not guarantee that David would be accepted by the pilots or passengers once he began work.

CHAPTER 10

RAISE THE FLAPS

✈

David grabbed his black leather flight bag and boarded a plane to Dallas to begin flight training at the American Airlines headquarters. As he settled into his seat, all he wanted to do was relax, read a magazine, and spend some quiet time preparing for what he was worried would be the most demanding and most uncertain training experience of his life. If he was successful, he'd be able to have a career doing what he loved. If he failed, it would be catastrophic for his family and for the future of Black pilots. David had only a brief moment of silence in his seat. A chatty guy named Gus, with a deep southern drawl, sat next to David and started to converse.

They began the kind of casual chatting traveling strangers often have. It didn't take long before they learned they were both former military pilots, and both on the way to start training with American Airlines. Even more surprising, they were almost exactly the same age. Their birthdays were only days apart. Gus chatted on and on, continuing to pepper David with questions.

David prided himself on always being polite and didn't want to come across as rude, but he wished Gus would stop asking so many personal questions. David continued to answer graciously even as the questioning became more aggressive, as if it were an interrogation. As soon as they landed, David got off the plane and hurried ahead to their hotel, hoping to put some distance between himself and the talkative Gus.

For the three-month-long new pilot training, the airline housed new employees in a modest hotel. David would lodge there while Lyn and their children stayed with family in Ohio. David got to the hotel to find his room equipped with two beds, a desk, a lamp, and plain white walls. He figured that he would be assigned a roommate. There was no time to wonder about whom it would be: Gus walked right in and asked David to share a room.

"We can cooperate and graduate together!" Gus said.

David agreed, even as he realized that in all the questioning there was one thing Gus hadn't asked him, and that was about his race.

"Gus thought I was white," David recalled.

David walked straight-faced into the flight training room. On that first day of training, December 3, 1964, now fully employed by American Airlines, he felt a quiet pride at his accomplishment. Not only was he the first Black pilot at this company, he was the only African American pilot flying for a major commercial airline in America.

But even as his chest filled with pride, he wondered what to expect from his fellow pilots. He chose to say little during his early days of training, going about his day as the professional he was, even as he sensed he was being ignored. Where Gus had had a lot of questions for David, the other new pilots stayed silent and kept him at a distance. Heading from one class to another, David walked the hallways alone. He found himself feeling just as he had when he started as a young pilot trainee in the military.

One day, a week into the training, David sat in the hallway reviewing his flight manual when a pilot walked by.

"Hello," David said, smiling. He hoped he could make at least one strong relationship. He had to keep trying.

But this pilot, like so many others he'd met that first week, continued to walk. David looked down and let out a sigh. How long would this continue?

David needed someone to talk to about all this, and he missed Lyn. There were no cell phones or emails, no texting, no instant messaging, no video chats. He tried to call Lyn, but worried about being overheard. So, David picked up a pen. In the evenings after dinner, he would write letters to his wife explaining this new job and asking for advice.

There was one thing David really needed to talk to Lyn about: his roommate, Gus. At first, while it was hard to find a quiet moment in their room, something David craved, things were OK between the two. But then, Gus's behavior started to change. "Every day, after the

Black maids would clean up our room, Gus would have a bunch of nasty things to say about them," David recalled. "He would often call them the N-word and make a lot of disparaging remarks about them because they were Black."

David decided to say nothing back to Gus. He was sure everyone else had figured out by then that he was Black. Hadn't Gus too? David decided not to talk about race or ask Gus directly and instead vowed to focus on his work. Only his work.

After studying one night, David turned off the lights and lay in bed listening to one of his favorite singers, Ella Fitzgerald, a popular Black jazz musician, on his radio.

"Gus got up in the dark, and with a vengeance he turned off the radio and shouted, "'That's enough of that nigger!'" David recalled.

David, startled and confused, wasn't sure how to respond. He didn't want to overreact.

"I wanted to make a good impression, and I wanted to be a good pilot so other young Black pilots could follow in my footsteps. I didn't want to make a scene and complain to my new boss already," David said. "Would they say, 'So we hire a Black pilot and he's already a problem'? I didn't want the chief pilot to think I was a troublemaker or a complainer. He had already taken a chance on hiring me, and I didn't want him to think I was causing trouble."

His roommate's racist actions and words were terrible. To quietly endure this disrespect would be incredibly difficult. David wasn't sure how to react. He thought of the newspaper stories about protesters across the South who were advocates for racial equality and social change. He knew he would never protest like them, by closing down a street, leading a crowd, or rioting. He wasn't going to shout or throw punches because he was not a confrontational person. But he did want to do the right thing. He just had to figure out what was best and how he could make a difference from within the airline.

As he turned over the options in his mind, he considered the actions of the three young men who volunteered for the voter registration drive during "Freedom Summer" in 1964. The three had rallied to get more Black voters enrolled and led the charge to help make that happen. But then something horrible occurred: They disappeared.

Michael Schwerner, Andrew Goodman, and James Earl Chaney were driving to Meridian, Mississippi, when they vanished. In the fall, their bodies were found: They had been shot and buried beneath a dam.

David knew protesting or taking a stand could mean putting your life at risk. While he didn't think he'd be killed at work, he was keenly aware that Black people were targets, especially across Mississippi and Texas, where he now stayed in a hotel room with a man who certainly seemed to agree with white supremacists.

David thought about confronting Gus. But he did not want to make waves with his fellow pilots, particularly so early on during training.

Their shared hotel room became a difficult place to

study. David's resentment and anger swelled as he swallowed his pride again and again in the face of Gus's casual hateful commentary. Sometimes he got so exasperated with Gus's hatred, David was tempted to report him. Other times, he considered throwing a punch, which would surely stop the comments right then and there. But then David would take a step back. It wasn't what Dr. King would do. It wasn't what the Tuskegee Airmen would do. It wasn't what David wanted to do. And he had a family who depended on him. He had to be strong for them, and a lot depended on David getting it right. A lot depended on David keeping his cool and keeping his job.

While David pored over his books, Gus would pop off with racist remarks about Black people. "I would just keep reading and studying until my anger went away." David said.

When David wrote to Lyn asking for advice, he confided his feelings too. Lyn read each letter and responded but was secretly terrified for her husband. She even wondered if Gus was trying to get David riled up so he would be fired.

Weeks passed with David trying to manage this tense and awkward roommate relationship. Often after flight training, some of the white pilots would gather for dinner. David was never invited, and he never asked to be included.

One night, the others went to dinner, and, as usual, David stayed home. But the next day some pilots were buzzing about what happened at dinner. A former Air Force colleague filled him in.

Some of David's classmates were talking when one shouted what he thought was groundbreaking news: "I hear American Airlines hired a Black pilot!"

"Who?!" the classmates asked. "Who?!"

"DAVID HARRIS!" the student yelled back. "It's DAVID HARRIS!"

Apparently, Gus had nearly fallen out of his chair at the revelation.

But then Gus, perhaps in some misplaced attempt to defend David, said, "David ain't no nigger! We study together and we wash our clothes together! He ain't no nigger!"

Gus may have been embarrassed that he was living with a Black roommate, sleeping across the room from him every night. A man he thought was white was actually Black.

As David had suspected, it turned out that Gus didn't only dislike Black music or Black culture. He didn't like Black people at all.

The two stayed roommates until Gus's wife moved to Dallas. As soon as she arrived, Gus transferred into an apartment to live with her.

David breathed a sigh of relief. He stayed in the hotel room alone, where he no longer had to worry about his antagonistic roommate.

"All Black people navigate a delicate balance in the workplace, and David was no different," Lyn said.

"Throughout his career, our evenings were too often spent recounting what was said at work that made David bite his tongue or contain his anger."

Slowly but surely, some of his colleagues eventually began to accept David, and some even came to respect him. They began to say hello to David in the hallways; some would sit at the lunch table with him. They didn't all become good friends, but they weren't sworn enemies either.

The last day of flight training, David felt a sense of accomplishment. He was ready to get to work. But he kept his enthusiasm to himself as he received his first assignment.

"Congratulations," David's flight instructor said. "You're being assigned to Boston, effective immediately."

Days later, David boarded his first flight as a pilot with American Airlines. He'd been assigned to work as a co-pilot flying a Boeing 727—and he was ecstatic. Sure, he would navigate the same skies as he had when he was in the military, but there was something obviously different. In place of the stress of carrying weapons and being ready to fly into battle, David was now responsible for the safety of thousands of passengers. But he was up to the task. In contrast to the tenseness of his previous job, he would now greet passengers with babies; people who were flying to weddings, family reunions, job interviews, vacations, funerals, birthdays, anniversaries, and retirement parties. The atmosphere would be very different.

———————————————✈

Walking into Flight Operations, the room where pilots and flight attendants gathered before and after their flights to check their schedules, rest, and catch up with one another, David once again felt like the new kid at school. This was his first official workday as a first officer for American Airlines.

Everyone seemed busy doing something, and for a minute he couldn't decide what he should do. Then the chief pilot called out to him, "David, your captain's over there," using his pen to point to one corner of the room where a tall, lanky man with a bushy mustache seemed to be telling a funny story. Assuming this was the right man, David walked over, ready to introduce himself. Without breaking his rhythm, Captain Herb Macy turned to David, smiled, and said, "You like to fish?" Taken by surprise by the odd question, David hesitated and then said, "I think so."

Herb laughed and said, "I'll see you after the pre-flight." And with that greeting, David knew exactly what to do next: Go out to the plane and make sure it was ready to fly. After the exterior preflight, he walked up the stairs and into a new world. A steady stream of men, women, and a few children were chatting, looking for their seats, and greeting the flight attendants. Back then, they were called stewardesses, and were only women. Some glanced at David standing in the door of the cockpit. He wondered what they saw when they looked at him, but a few smiles put him at ease.

Herb joined him in the cockpit, and together they did the final preflight checks, closed the door, and got ready to roll. Barely airborne, Herb traded his captain's hat for a fishing cap and asked if David had ever had steamers.

"What are steamers?" David asked.

"Clams," Herb said. "Clams in a shell. They are very tasty. We'll eat some soon."

From that first flight onward, Herb invited David out for coffee, lunch, or dinner. They'd get together to talk about airplanes and aviation. Herb was older and soon became much more than a flight mentor.

"He took me under his wing," David said of Herb. "He became my friend."

Lyn said it was no coincidence that Herb ended up in the cockpit with David and became his mentor. David was taking a chance on American Airlines. But American Airlines was also taking a chance on David, and it didn't want any problems by teaming David with a pilot who was uncomfortable flying with a Black man. They had to work together as a team. The very safety of the passengers on board depended on it. The company knew Herb would be a great fit.

American Airlines got that right.

CHAPTER 11
GROUND CONTROL

✈

David and Lyn sat on a wooden bench at a table overlooking the bay on the South Shore of Massachusetts. Herb and his vivacious and very funny wife, Kit, sat across from them in a noisy Plymouth, Massachusetts, restaurant.

"Are you ready for steamers?" asked Herb.

David couldn't believe he was here, sitting in a New England restaurant across from this jolly descendant of Nantucket whalers, who seemed bent on showing him how to eat clams with his fingers. Becoming a commercial airline pilot had unexpectedly given him a whole new world of experiences.

"Here's how you do it," Herb said as a bowl full of slimy, snotty-looking gray clumps arrived at their table. David thought about pasta, pizza, and hamburgers, and wondered why on earth anyone would ever get excited about a bowl of clams.

Herb told David to use his fingers to pull the skin off the clams, discard the shells into a bowl, dip the clams into a cup of seawater to wash off the grit, then dip them into melted butter and eat them.

"I followed Herb's advice and did exactly what he did," David recalled. "They were delicious!"

Meanwhile, Lyn and Kit had been chatting while Lyn tentatively tried a few steamers. Then, in a fit of bravery, Lyn ordered the second lobster of her life. The first, ordered at the officers' club at one of their bases, had been sent back untouched because she couldn't figure out how to break into it.

This time, Herb, seeing her puzzled expression when the huge red crustacean was plunked down in front of her, simply leaned over, ripped off its tail, pulled out the succulent meat, and popped it into her bowl of butter. "There you go," he said with a happy grin, turning back to David's ongoing struggle with his steamers.

As soon as David and his family moved to the Boston area, Herb and Kit introduced them to New England culture, starting with food. Besides flying, eating was one of Herb's great passions, and David was happy to get on board. Over many meals and dozens and dozens of steamers, David slowly started to open up to Herb.

Herb was more than just a co-pilot and David's friend; he also exposed David to places where few African Americans ventured in New England. Having been raised in a middle-class family, David was accustomed to nice restaurants. But this was different. Herb's interests were things David had never experienced before. And

David knew that as he sat in this seaside restaurant surrounded by white customers, racial bigotry and the civil rights protests unfolded only a few miles away.

In 1964, Boston was, for all intents and purposes, rigidly segregated. Perhaps not by law, but certainly in practice. One section of the city was for upper-middle-class or wealthy white residents, and another was for Black people. Boston's school desegregation and busing crisis had gotten underway. There was a revolt among Black citizens against segregation in the public schools.

Because Lyn knew she and David had one chance to educate their girls, they had chosen to live in the suburbs, where more of the wealthier and better educated people resided, rather than in Boston proper, where Lyn knew that the school system would be difficult for Black students as desegregation plans ramped up.

But buying a house in Beverly, the middle-class suburb of Boston the Harrises had chosen, turned out to be more difficult than expected. Like other new pilots at American Airlines, David and Lyn wanted to buy a house based on the company's good, solid pay and to begin living the American dream. While it worked out exactly that way for David's co-workers, the Harrises' home loan was denied. They had been redlined, a common practice that denied loans requested by Black people attempting to buy houses in white neighborhoods. It was a system of segregation that contributed to decades of deep, persistent patterns of housing discrimination, the effects of which can still be felt today in some urban areas.

Distressed and not sure what to do, David told his chief pilot in Boston what had happened. Unlike many employers, David's company took the initiative and made a few strategic phone calls, and the bank reversed its denial, allowing the loan. The Harris family became homeowners.

Wary but determined, they moved into their modest ranch house, not sure what to expect from their neighbors. Generally, the people they met were friendly, and David, Lyn, and their small daughters began to settle into their first, post-military permanent home. It was several years later that Lyn learned that one neighbor had started a petition to try and prevent them from moving there. It was quashed by other residents who were horrified at this bigoted effort to keep their neighborhood "safely white."

As David settled into his job and their children into school, Lyn returned to college. Because she'd married at 18, her mother made her promise she'd finish college, and finally, at 25, she was determined to honor that pledge. While Lyn studied, David flew airplanes. On days off, they enjoyed being at home with their family. Not only was David a skilled aviator, but he was a talented builder too. He constructed a new swimming pool and bathroom for their house.

Lyn became active with the League of Women Voters and soon graduated from college. Her professional career took off when she was hired as a TV reporter and anchor working for a local television station. "Black people in Boston knew David and me from whatever press we got and from seeing me on TV," Lyn said.

Leslie was just a young girl when David started working for American Airlines, but she has vivid memories of riding in a Volkswagen Beetle, one of their first family cars. The Harrises spent a lot of time together on the road as they often made the 45-minute drive to Boston's Logan Airport to drop off or pick up David.

"My father was incredibly handy, and this being before car seats, he modified the back of the car so it would be easy to travel with two small children," Leslie said. "Dad removed the back seat and built a platform that created a sort of playpen or crib in the back of the car."

Because flights leave at all hours, the family would often drive to and from the airport in the dark of night. "Mom would bundle us up and lay me down in the back of the car, and we would head out. Lying in this playpen, I could see the streetlights from the car windows. I suppose this earliest memory in my life is also my earliest memory of my life with a barrier-breaking pilot for a father," Leslie said.

But while their home life felt more and more secure, David knew that racial issues were still a threat. Driving through white neighborhoods in Boston as a Black man during the mid-1960s could be very dangerous. Police brutality against Black people was a serious and valid concern.

Social justice activists accused the police of harshness and unjustified violence against Black citizens. They complained that the police were unresponsive to Black citizens, particularly after the beating and arrest of Roxbury resident and famous folk singer Jackie Washington. Many people felt he had been targeted by police because of his skin color.

And there were protests. Dr. King himself led a march from Roxbury to Boston Commons to rally against school segregation. It was an uneasy and unpredictable time. On the one hand, David and Lyn had moved to a white middle-class neighborhood where, after a tough start, they felt at home and part of the community. On the other hand, less than 30 minutes away, riots and protesters filled the streets in the name of racial equality, trying to get white people and Black people to live as equals.

At work, David walked through Boston's busy airport dressed neatly in his blue uniform and was greeted warmly by Black skycaps, the porters at the airport. David was a visible symbol of success and progress, and he knew the skycaps were proud of him. He returned their affection because that pride was never lost on him. He welcomed their support because even though he was highly skilled and experienced, he still felt he received surprised stares from skeptical white passengers who whispered their disapproval and pointed at him as he stepped into the cockpit.

As he had in the military, David again proved himself to be a competent and successful pilot. In under two years, he was promoted from first officer to captain. And soon after to check airman, a pilot who is qualified to conduct flight checks, which meant that David evaluated other pilots. It was perhaps ironic that David, a Black man, would be judging and evaluating white men in the sky while a pivotal moment in civil rights history unfolded on the ground below.

David was in the air during the historic Selma to Montgomery March on March 7, 1965. Demanding that they be allowed to register to vote, 600 protesters began a peaceful walk. But after only six blocks, the police attacked them with tear gas and beat the marchers with clubs, shutting down the protest. Images of this terrible mistreatment aired on televisions across the country, and the day became known as Bloody Sunday.

Like the brave protesters who marched in Alabama, David was on his own journey for equality. As the first Black commercial airline pilot, David hoped that with every smooth flight he could prove to the white pilots that he was just as competent and skilled, and that he deserved their respect.

TOP LEFT David posing for a photo with the tail of an American Airlines plane behind him; **TOP RIGHT** Lyn and David; **BOTTOM** A young David (second from right) with his fellow Air Force pilots

CAPTAIN DAVE HARRIS

FAR LEFT TOP David posing for a photo in the engine of an American Airlines plane; **FAR LEFT BOTTOM** David's wings from American Airlines; **TOP RIGHT** A plaque from a memorial group of the Tuskegee Airmen, David's heroes, honoring his contribution to aviation; **CENTER RIGHT** David's medal from the Black Aviation Hall of Fame; **BOTTOM RIGHT** David (far left) with fellow Black airline pilots in the cockpit of a plane

TOP David with his father, Wilbur
BOTTOM David, in his 80s, next to his plane
at his home in North Carolina

CHAPTER 12

DISTRESSED DESCENT

✈

David gripped the yoke and, with the runway in sight, lowered the landing gear as he prepared to touch down at National Airport. He peered out of the small rectangular, airtight window and saw bright orange flames burst around Washington, D.C.

His stomach churned. He knew the reason for the fires: His hero, Dr. Martin Luther King, Jr., had been assassinated.

David had seen wildfires in the Midwest. He'd flown over brush fires on the West Coast. He knew how to fly above smoke, but he knew these fires were different. These flames were coming from the city itself, which meant there was serious unrest on the streets of the nation's capital. From the sky, and with nearly 80 passengers on board, David watched neighborhoods burn. Flames engulfed buildings. Plumes of dark smoke filled the air. And while he couldn't see it from up high, he knew there was rioting in some parts of the city.

It only made sense that David would witness another key moment of history from the sky. From that great height, he watched the urban rebellion that would go on to span four days in Washington, D.C. More than 100 cities across the country experienced demonstrations and civil unrest in response to Dr. King's assassination. Angry protesters, horrified by the injustice of his death, lit fire to whatever they could find to burn. By the end of that summer in 1968, 39 people nationwide would die in the riots.

David understood all too well the racial discrimination that Black people experienced on a daily basis. As a pilot, he also knew he had a responsibility to put his feelings aside and land the airplane safely.

Dr. King had always been one of David's greatest heroes, a beacon of hope for a more equal future, and so he was deeply saddened and angry about Dr. King's murder. Even though he understood how people could be so furious, he was still shocked to see the fires and violence that ensued. But it was what happened next that really stunned him.

"We were on final approach when my white co-pilot began to criticize Dr. King," David recalled. "He said, 'It's good King got killed!'"

At first, David couldn't believe what he was hearing. But the co-pilot emphatically repeated his words, expressing his glee over the death of this man who had preached nonviolence and peace.

They were minutes from landing with a plane full of passengers on board, and David was enraged. He started to shake. Images and memories flashed through his mind. He thought of Black men casually being called "boy" as a way to demean them—Black people who had swallowed their pride countless times, and who had been beaten, lynched, and systematically dehumanized and mistreated.

As his co-pilot nonchalantly spewed his hatred and callousness, David suddenly felt that this co-pilot was emblematic of the problem in the United States. It seemed to David that it was this almost willful, spiteful lack of empathy for another person or group that prevented reconciliation, understanding, and opening hearts and minds to different views. Instead, it created resentment and anger. But how can anyone undo some-one's upbringing? How can anyone help people reframe the way they think? Certainly not on a 20-minute landing.

A professional first and foremost, David breathed and focused on landing the 78,000-pound airplane. The BAC-111 made it safely to the ground. David taxied to the gate and shut down the engines. He waited for all the passengers to leave the airplane, and then he leaned over in the cockpit, close to his co-pilot.

His words were precise and firm and eerily calm. David told his co-pilot that he didn't want to hear any more of his mean-spirited remarks about Dr. King, a man of peace. And he told the co-pilot he would never fly with him again.

And he didn't.

David left the airport and checked into a small hotel in Washington, D.C., finding a safe place, miles away from the riots. He was tired. Tired after a long day of work, tired of the racial unrest that engulfed America, and tired of having to defend himself, and Dr. King, in his own cockpit.

CHAPTER 13

WIND SHEAR

✈

Buildings smoldered, city streets filled with demonstrators, and the nation continued to reel from the riots that followed Dr. King's assassination. David, meanwhile, flew in and out of Washington, D.C., and Boston, watching it all unfold from the air.

While David did his job, Lyn faced her own problems as the mother of the only two Black children in an otherwise white elementary school. She felt her daughters were subjected to subtle racism that required more than one trip to talk to teachers about their attitudes and behaviors toward her small daughters. As she drove past a group of boys on one of those trips, her windows down, she heard the word "nigger." Backing up, she said, "What did you say?" At that, the boys ran. "We were jumpy," Lyn remembered. "But we went about our lives the best we could."

Weeks later, with memories from the D.C. riots still fresh, David sat at a table in the American Airlines lunchroom in Dallas.

What had America learned from Dr. King's death, David wondered. Dr. King was this incredible leader who had preached nonviolence and love and reconciliation and forgiveness. And his life had been taken from him. Perhaps this tragic event was the wake-up call the nation needed. Perhaps ideologies would finally change.

Beside him at the lunch table, a white pilot took a bite of his sandwich. And with ease, just as the racist co-pilot had days earlier, he too joked about Dr. King's assassination.

"He was laughing about it," David recalled. "He said, 'Every nigger I passed on the street was crying because King got killed.'" David added: "He thought it was funny and that cut me like a knife."

Some of the pilots looked up to watch David's reaction. He was certain others privately hoped he'd storm out of the room and quit.

But David wasn't a quitter.

Like so many times before, David swallowed his anger. Thinking about how his family depended on him, he tried to show restraint and not make any hasty decisions. He also knew that this one loud-mouthed person's opinion wasn't everyone's.

He thought of Cami and Leslie, who beamed with pride when David was able to take them on one of his flights. They got to fly nearly for free and sit in first class. They wore fancy dresses with plastic wings pinned to their neat lapels, eating ice-cream sundaes and wiping their chocolate-sticky faces with warm towels while flight attendants gushed.

He remembered how proud Cami was of him when the passengers on board clapped after one of his perfect landings. And how interested his girls seemed when he'd take them into the cockpit to explain what he did as the captain, and what the co-pilot and flight engineer did on takeoff and landing. He'd shown them that it was possible to achieve something great. Hopefully they understood, too, that their dad was paving the way for other Black pilots to follow—that holding this position meant a great step toward achieving equality in the workplace, and elsewhere. Certainly, his girls understood how much their dad loved to fly.

DAVID WALKED AWAY FROM THE LAUGHTER IN THE LUNCHROOM WITHOUT UTTERING A WORD.

Thinking of Dr. King, thinking of his girls, David focused on how much he wanted to have equality between races in the skies as he did on land. But if he were fired, there would be segregated skies for years to come.

So David walked away from the laughter in the lunchroom without uttering a word. He held his head high, suppressed his rage, and prepared for his next flight.

CHAPTER 14

ESSENTIAL POWER

✈

The Boeing 727 from Boston to Dallas was completely full, with 150 passengers on board. David sat in the pilot seat with his hands gently gripping the yoke, flying the plane as it climbed to 30,000 feet. The flight attendants let him know that they were preparing to serve dinner.

Somewhere near Hartford, Connecticut, his flight engineer looked over at him. "Dave, we're losing oil on the number three engine!"

David knew this would require his serious attention. The 727 has three engines and oil loss could signal a hydraulics problem, which could not be repaired in flight.

What would he do? Where was the closest airport to land? He might need to land with his jet engines shut down.

During emergency situations, David had to rely on his lessons from flight school, the many hours spent in an airplane simulator, the thousands of hours in the air flying passengers from coast to coast, and something intangible that can't be taught in simulators for split-second decisions.

On the 727 airplanes, "essential" power, like flight instruments, can be switched to any of the three noisy 4,700-pound JT8D turbofan engines. Normally, the essential power is carried on the number three engine.

"Do you think it's a gauge failure or are we really losing the oil?" David asked his flight engineer.

"It looks like an authentic oil loss at the rate that the needle is going down," the flight engineer replied.

Without looking at a manual, David ordered in a calm and steady tone, "Go ahead and put the essential power on the number one engine."

He called air traffic control to report the emergency situation. He decided to turn the airplane around and head back to Boston. And he told the flight attendants not to start serving dinner. After David entered a new flight plan back to Boston, all was going well—until the flight engineer spoke up again.

"Hey, Dave," the flight engineer said, "we're losing oil in the number two engine now. So we're losing oil on the number three engine and the number two engine!"

"Oh my god. The number three engine is running at reduced power, we haven't shut it down yet, and now we're losing oil on the number two engine!" David said. "This is a real problem!"

They had already moved the essential flight instruments to the number one engine, which was operating fine. But he thought through his next move and gave another order to his flight engineer: "Watch the oil pressure and temperature," David said. "If the temperature starts to rise, immediately shut off the number three engine!"

In a blink of an eye, David made a critical decision: He shut down the number three engine before it overheated. David and his crew were getting closer to Boston.

"We were on final approach and we were down to two engines. And engine two was losing lots of oil," David recalled.

They were only a few miles from the runway when David lowered the landing gear. The runway was in sight as lights flashed on the instrument panel. David knew he needed to land the airplane soon.

Over the loudspeaker, David told the flight attendants and passengers to prepare for landing. He checked the altimeter and guided the airplane downward—10,000 feet, 5,000 feet, 1,000 feet, a smooth landing.

"We got to the gate, shut all the engines down, and left the cockpit to check the outside of the airplane. Both engines were covered in oil," David said.

A team of well-trained mechanics moved quickly to clean off the engines on the tarmac and fixed the problem while the passengers remained on the airplane. David explained the situation to the passengers, put them at ease, and they all decided to stay on board.

"We didn't lose a single passenger," David said. "And

we got to Dallas only 40 minutes late!"

David provided those passengers, and so many others, with a safe flight. During his career with American Airlines, he'd go on to reassure other passengers and even inspire some to pursue flight themselves. Belinda Smith-Sullivan only needed two words to explain why she became a pilot: David Harris.

Until she met David, Belinda never thought she could fly. But Belinda, an African American woman with a quick smile, went on to earn her pilot's license and then buy a twin-engine, four-seat airplane and compete in cross-country air races.

The two met in the early 1970s when she was a flight attendant for American Airlines. Short, wisp-like, and a fast talker, she had been working for about six months when, on a flight from Dallas, one of her fellow attendants told her there was a Black pilot in the cockpit.

She didn't believe it.

If it was true, Belinda knew she was witnessing history. She returned to the galley in the rear of the airplane and started asking the other flight attendants questions: How long had David been a pilot? When did he become a captain? Was he friendly?

Belinda had ever only dreamed that a Black man could someday be a pilot. Little did she know that by meeting David, she too would expand her dreams and achieve things beyond anything she'd imagined.

She developed a kinship with David because he was Black and also because he understood a bit of what she was going through. Racial segregation had extended to flight attendants, too, dating back to 1963, when Joan Dorsey became the first African American in that role, also for American Airlines.

Joan graduated at the top of her class of what was then known as Stewardess College. She was the first African American at American Airlines to be promoted to a supervisory position within Flight Services. She retired after 36 years of service. During her working years, she encountered pilots who didn't allow Black flight attendants in the cockpit and passengers who didn't want Black flight attendants to serve them. Joan had been through a lot, and she'd paved the way for Belinda's career. Belinda understood that David was doing the same for future Black pilots.

Months went by and Belinda continued to work on David's flights. Each time, she got a thrill watching David excel at his job. She saw him put anxious passengers at ease, especially those who suffered from a fear of flying.

On one flight from Dallas to Boston, a member of the American Airlines crew told David before the flight took off that a passenger was so nervous about flying that she trembled in her seat.

"I walked back to her seat, and I asked her if she was all right," David said. "She was very nervous and afraid, so I asked her to come with me to the cockpit."

David asked the co-pilot to step away and invited the passenger to sit in the co-pilot's seat. "I showed her all the flight instruments, pointed them out, and told her that the airplane was completely safe because there was redundancy in safety equipment. I told her that it's safer to fly than it is to drive a car. I answered all of her questions and walked her back to her seat, and the flight attendants said she had a great flight."

David became a friend to Belinda, and a teacher. "David encouraged me to fly," Belinda said. "I bought my own airplane because of David's influence, and I've been flying ever since."

CHAPTER 15

ALL-BLACK
FLIGHT CREW

✈

irst came the stares.

David noticed the travelers in the bustling airport whispering, pointing, and gawking at him. Many of them looked surprised. Dozens seemed laser-focused on David and his flight crew, all pilots walking together through Dallas–Fort Worth International Airport, one of the busiest airports in the world.

It was May 20, 1984, and they looked sharp. All three wore well-pressed blue American Airlines uniforms and crisp blue pilot's hats, and carried a small black leather flight bag.

But why were these pilots so different? Why the stares?

They were all African Americans.

The opportunity to fly with two other Black pilots was accidental. As a check airman, David could fly in the place of any assigned pilot. In the process of looking for a flight he needed as part of his flying requirements, he decided to see where his good friend Herman "Sam"

Samuels was headed. He was in luck. Their schedules matched. David rounded up Sam and made the necessary crew changes.

Then Jim Greene, another one of the few African American pilots in the system, walked in. He looked at David, then at Sam and said, "You two flying together?"

"Yes, we are," said David with enthusiasm.

Then Jim said, "Do you realize if I go with you, we've got an all-Black crew?"

In that moment, David knew he was about to make history again. "We put it together. We made it happen."

Sam had worked for American Airlines for eight years before becoming a pilot. He started in hourly positions in all kinds of airport operations, including handling baggage, ticketing, and working in ramp and fleet services. But he had always wanted to fly. So he took extra shifts and moonlighted as a taxi driver to earn more income. During his time off, he took flying lessons. "The people I worked with told me all the time, 'You are wasting your time. American Airlines is not going to give you a job as a pilot.' That was just fuel to me," he said.

David met Sam when he was a baggage handler and encouraged him to pursue his pilot's license. Sam, who would go on to earn the rank of captain and work at the airline for 30 years, became the first African American pilot to fly for American Airlines who had not been trained in the military.

David looked at his flight crew and, sizing up the significance of this event, slowed down. He took his time walking through the airport to savor the moment. This wasn't a random stroll; it was a walk through time. It was a walk to honor the Tuskegee Airmen who flew before David, Sam, and Jim. And it was also a walk for the many Black pilots who would soar the skies after that day.

David couldn't stop smiling. He nodded pleasantly to the passengers in the terminal, as if he were giving them permission to stare.

It didn't matter if some of the passengers disapproved of the all-Black crew. The three men were proud to be there together. They'd earned it. This moment didn't belong to those who stared. It belonged to the three tall, dignified Black men dressed impeccably in blue uniforms, strolling into history.

IT WAS A **WALK TO HONOR** THE TUSKEGEE AIRMEN WHO FLEW BEFORE DAVID, SAM, AND JIM.

Passengers in the terminal all seemed to notice that these men were heading in the same direction, past the flight check-in desk and straight to the door of the jet bridge.

The door was locked.

Silence.

It became absolutely quiet in the gate area where the passengers focused on the three Black pilots and the locked door.

Were these pilots actually flying this huge Boeing 727?

"I put the key in the door of the jet bridge and

opened it," David recalled, "and all three of us walked down together as the passengers craned their necks to watch."

"Did you see that?" they heard one passenger ask. "They all got on our airplane!"

"We kept our faces straight," David said. "We were very professional, but once we got in the cockpit and closed the door, we laughed, enjoying the moment."

"We turned a lot of heads," Sam said. "One Black pilot back then was a novelty, but three Black pilots walking to the same gate ... well, that was historic! I'm sure there were some passengers who questioned whether they made the right decision by booking that flight."

After the crew completed their lengthy preflight checklist and double-checked their flight instruments, David opened the cockpit door. "Everyone who boarded the airplane could peek into the cockpit and see the three of us preparing for takeoff," David said. "Heads were spinning."

For the first time, an all-Black flight crew taxied to an active runway, steered the airplane off the ground to 30,000 feet, guided the airplane to final approach, touched down smoothly, parked at the gate, shut down the engines, and celebrated a historic moment—together.

CHAPTER 16

FINAL APPROACH

David didn't want to retire. He loved flying and took deep pride in his stellar career as a pilot.

He was a meticulous preflight aviator and kind to all the crew, chatting with airline mechanics on the tarmac before every flight.

David relished the rush of guiding big airplanes into the sky, and he also looked forward to interacting with passengers before takeoff. He liked standing in front of the cockpit to greet passengers before flights, and he would usually find a way to say goodbye when they departed too. His calming presence often put anxious passengers at ease. And they liked talking to him. Some would tell him about their travels, families, and marriages, and show him pictures of their babies. He didn't want any of that to end.

But on December 1, 1994, David double-checked his flight plan while sitting in the cockpit of an MD-11, a three-engine wide-body, and prepared for his last trip with American Airlines. He had reached the maximum retirement age, after 30 years as a pilot, in what to him seemed like the blink of an eye.

He had survived six and half years in the Air Force preparing for war; he had battled blatant racism in the military and as a civilian; he had flown hundreds of thousands of miles in some of America's largest state-of-the-art airplanes; he had earned the title of the first Black pilot hired by a major commercial airline, received his promotion to captain, and served as a trailblazer for other Black pilots who wanted to follow in his footsteps. David was a national role model. He was respected in the airline industry. Journalists called to chronicle his story. And now, he couldn't believe that when this trip ended, his career would too.

As a child, Leslie recalled, she had no idea how important and monumental her father's career was in the history of aviation—or, for that matter, as an accomplished professional Black man in America.

"Only when I got older and started to see him through the eyes of people in the industry who revered him, and through the eyes of young people who aspired to be like him, did I start to understand what a hero he is," she said. "To me, he was always just Dad. What I see in him now is that he did not choose to fly to be the first, to

> DAVID WAS A **NATIONAL** ROLE MODEL. HE WAS **RESPECTED** IN THE AIRLINE INDUSTRY.

blaze trails, or to get into history books. He chose to fly because he loves to fly."

David was reluctant to leave the cockpit for good, but instead of becoming upset, he prepared to celebrate the milestone. He had become a legend at American Airlines. For Black pilots, David was a big brother, a mentor, a friend, and a confidant. They all looked up to him, and they respected him, followed his lead, and praised him for making their aviation careers possible.

David's last trip was from Miami, Florida, to Buenos Aires, Argentina, with a side round trip to Santiago, Chile, before returning from Buenos Aires. He would depart Miami at night and arrive in Buenos Aires the next morning and check into a hotel. The following day, he would fly over the mountains to Santiago, then back to Buenos Aires to spend another night, and then the following evening fly overnight back to Miami, where he would say goodbye to his flight crew for the last time. When the landing gear of that last flight lowered, he'd be a retiree.

"Traditionally, on your last trip as a captain, the airline tries to make you feel good and do little things for you," David recalled. "They would usually make a big sheet cake to share with the crew and some of the passengers."

But that never happened. David's flight out of Miami was delayed, and in the hectic hours trying to leave Florida, the crew wasn't able to get a cake. David eventually took off and flew from Miami to Buenos Aires.

FOR BLACK PILOTS, DAVID WAS A BIG BROTHER, A MENTOR, A FRIEND, AND A CON- FIDANT.

During the flight, he tried to hide his disappointment in not having a celebration by conjuring thoughts about his many amazing and historic flights spanning three decades. He reflected on one of his most memorable flights, the one on which, by chance, he met one of his civil rights heroes.

It was in the 1960s and David was the captain on a BAC-111. Since there was no jet bridge back then, he watched from the cockpit as passengers walked up the steps and onto the airplane. Suddenly, David saw a man he recognized: It was Whitney Young, the charismatic executive director of the National Urban League and a civil rights icon.

"I stepped out of the cockpit when he reached the top of the stairs, and I said, 'Hello, Mr. Young, I am Captain David Harris. Welcome aboard!'" said David. Then he went on to say, "Thank you for all the work you are doing for civil rights. It is work like yours and others' that has made it possible for me to secure this job."

Young simply said, "Thank you," David recalled, and walked to his seat.

Under Young's direction, the National Urban League grew from 60 to 98 chapters. The league advocated against discrimination and was responsible for overseeing racial integration in corporate workplaces, including large companies like American Airlines. Young went on to become a consultant on racial issues to Presidents Kennedy and Johnson.

Years later, in 1971, Young drowned. He was only 49

years old. Young's wife, Margaret, asked American Airlines executives to provide the charter airplane to carry Young's body from the funeral in New York to the burial in Kentucky, and she specifically asked that David fly the charter flight.

"Mr. Young must have mentioned me to his wife," David recalled. "I was flattered that she requested I fly the charter. It was an honor."

That flight carried many of America's most influential Black civil rights leaders and professionals: Roy Wilkins, a former leader of the NAACP; Reverend Jesse Jackson; Andrew Young, who would one day become ambassador to the United Nations; James Forman, a onetime leader of the Student Nonviolent Coordinating Committee (SNCC); and journalist Carl Rowan, among others.

As David left the house, Lyn, chuckling at the irony of the situation, reminded him of the importance of his mission: "For goodness sake, don't screw this up," she said. "You'll wipe out the entire civil rights movement!"

That flight was one of the things that influenced how David saw his role within the movement. David saw that he could fight for equality in the workplace in his own way. He could work behind the scenes to push his agenda forward. It was after seeing those leaders that he became more vocal at work about equality. Years later, he'd even get the chance to sit down with then CEO Bob Crandall to urge him to hire more African American pilots. Maybe it had been at his suggestion, or maybe it had been because David had done such good work. Whatever the reason, American now had more Black pilots.

David knew this was all for the best. He believed a more diverse workforce would help improve race relations because white and Black people, by working together, could learn to like each other, or at least learn to respect one another.

Lyn described David's contribution to the civil rights movement as subtle but significant: "He never tried to hide his Blackness while achieving success in his career. He doesn't have a temper. He was steady and focused on what he had to do to become a good pilot." To become a success.

> HE BELIEVED A MORE **DIVERSE** WORKFORCE WOULD HELP IMPROVE RACE RELATIONS ...

The memory of that charter flight with civil rights leaders, and the steps he'd taken after it, filled him with pride. And as David sat in the cockpit on his retirement flight and looked over his flight plan, he reflected on another milestone flight from his years in the air. This one was more personal, a flight that he took with his dad years earlier.

David's father, Wilbur Harris, was a quiet, soft-spoken man. Although David and his dad enjoyed a strong relationship, Wilbur was not warm or affectionate. He wasn't big on hugging, and he never told David that he was proud of him. But David knew his father cared.

"My dad was not very demonstrative or exuberant. He was very quiet; he was smart," David said. "I learned a lot from him."

In the mid-1980s, as his father's health declined, David invited his dad to join him on a flight to Madrid, Spain. David was the captain of a Boeing 767, a twin-engine wide-body and one of the first aircraft with a glass cockpit and state-of-the-art digital flight deck instruments.

David got his dad settled in a comfortable first-class seat. Once the plane had reached 35,000 feet and had started to cross the Atlantic Ocean, David went to check on his father. Dressed in his neat blue airline uniform and hat, he walked to the first-class cabin and leaned over his dad. "Are you having a good time?" he asked. "What do you think of this flight?"

And then something unforeseen happened. "My dad grabbed my hand, looked at me, and for the first time, he said: 'I am so proud of you,'" David said.

"I didn't know if I was going to make it back to the cockpit because it was so emotional for me," David recalled. "It was the first time my dad had ever said something like that to me."

"I tried to let my emotions wear off, and then I found my way back to the cockpit," David recalled. "I know my co-pilot wondered what was wrong with me!"

Lyn summed it up: "I think David had been waiting his entire life for any sign of love and approval from his father. It meant everything to him."

David's last trip with American was coming to an end. He'd landed in Buenos Aires after the round trip to Santiago, and after a rest, it was time to return to Miami to complete the itinerary, ending his 30-year career as a commercial pilot.

As David walked into the cockpit and prepared to depart Buenos Aires, he was greeted with a big surprise: The cockpit was decorated with flowers, balloons, and crepe paper.

Settling in, he heard a voice in his headset speaking from the control tower: "There's a brief delay. But you can push back shortly."

David used the delay to do another safety check, to review the flight controls again, and to think of the people he'd worked with outside the cockpit. Over the years, he'd established strong relationships with ground crews in the United States and overseas, the people who fuel the airplanes, the men and women who guide the planes to the gate, the baggage handlers, the people who clean the airplanes—folks who provide important operational services on the ground but who often go unnoticed to passengers. To David, these people were indispensable.

From the cockpit, high off the ground, he went over his checklist and prepared to push back from the gate. The long runway was dimly lit.

"Captain, you've got clearance for pushback," said a voice from the control tower.

"Roger," David replied. He released the brakes of the

MD-11 and slowly pushed back from the gate. What happened next left David speechless.

"I looked down over the nose of the airplane and there was the entire ground crew from Buenos Aires, everybody I had a relationship with, standing under the nose of the airplane and waving goodbye to me."

"I could barely crank the engines," David said. "Tears came to my eyes; they were waving and showing me so much love. It was much better than a cake, I thought. But then a cake appeared too. The ground crew and flight attendants had arranged for the cake in Buenos Aires. It was so large, it was enough to serve to the crew and the passengers."

When the time came to guide the MD-11 into the sky toward Argentina's Sierra de la Ventana mountains, David felt a surge of joy and sadness.

HE WAS OFFICIALLY RETIRED ...

The lights on the runway faded, and he could no longer see the ground.

Hours later, he safely landed the airplane in Miami, shook hands with the crew, and said goodbye to people he had worked with for decades. Scattered across the cockpit floor were tiny pieces of colorful crepe paper and a few flower petals, a small reminder of David's last piloted flight.

He was officially retired and now just another airline passenger trying to get home. Carrying his leather flight bag, David waited in the Miami airport gate area for his flight home to Boston.

He looked out the large window facing the tarmac and watched the airplane he had just landed push back from the gate with a new pilot in the cockpit.

As he wiped tears from his eyes, it set in: David's commercial career was over.

"Boarding all passengers for Boston," the airline gate agent blared.

David walked slowly down the crowded jet bridge, stood in line with all the other passengers, and pondered his future.

What would David do now?

EPILOGUE

✈

David crouches in the cockpit of his blue, white, and gold Socata Trinidad airplane and listens to the spinning blades of the stainless steel propeller.

He pays close attention to the buzzing sounds as each blade spins quickly, triggering puffs of air at the end of each turn. David is concerned about a potential problem with the propeller, which needs to be repaired. He sits on the sturdy wing and detects the faint smell of oil.

"Hey, David, how's it going?!" a neighbor shouts as he drives by.

"I'm getting this plane airworthy!" David replies.

David's Trinidad is parked in his driveway outside his airplane hangar. These days he lives in a laid-back rural airpark community in South Carolina, where every house has a hangar, where every home has a pilot, and where every paved street is a winding route to the runway.

David knows most of his neighbors by name, he knows how long they've been pilots, and he is familiar with the models of their airplanes. He can tell you when some of their airplanes were purchased, and he knows the quiet neighbor who spent months building his own airplane from a mail-order kit.

Many years have passed since David's retirement: He now mentors young people who are considering aviation as a career, he speaks to kids at local schools, and in 2018, he was honored by a Tuskegee Airmen memorial group in David's hometown of Columbus, Ohio. In 2019, he was honored by Sisters of the Skies, a national organization of Black female pilots, which presented David with an award to acknowledge his distinguished career.

"When I was hired with American Airlines in 1964, the only Black person I saw was my own reflection in the mirror," David told the group. "But today I am so happy to look around the room and see so many accomplished Black female pilots."

Most mornings these days, David's neighbors know where to find him: At a busy diner off Route 20 in South Carolina, about 15 minutes from his house.

"Good morning, David!" a shout comes from the grill where the cook is making hash brown potatoes and pancakes. "How are you?"

"I'm great," David says. "And looking forward to some of your good coffee."

"Good to see you again, Dave!" says the diner's manager, a friendly white man wearing a white apron and a wide smile. "We have a booth ready for you."

Everyone at the diner knows David. He's treated like

an honored guest. He never waits long for a booth, if at all, and he knows all the waitresses by name.

Gone are the days from 60 years ago when a white manager of a small-town Florida diner told David that he couldn't even sit inside his restaurant because he was Black.

That was then.

Today, at this diner in South Carolina, David eats breakfast in peace. While racism has not been erased from America, great strides have been made, laws passed, and on this sunny morning, David sits in his favorite diner knowing he won't be harassed because of the color of his skin.

"We really like David here," the waitress whispers to a visitor.

From the diner, or from his back porch overlooking his green, freshly mowed lawn, David listens to the airplanes circling his neighborhood and can say with certainty if the airplane is a single-engine or twin-engine.

In his home office, trophies, letters of recognition, and plaques adorn his walls, paying tribute to his heroes and his own remarkable career. There's a photo of Guion S. Bluford, Jr., the first African American astronaut to travel into space, and another photo with members of the famed Tuskegee Airmen.

How did those years pass by so fast? David wonders. He has accomplished so much as an aviator—and as a Black aviator: He was a captain in the U.S. Air Force flying B-52 bombers, the world's largest and most expensive airplane at the time. He became a captain with American Airlines, flying sophisticated and technologically advanced airplanes. He smiles broadly while thinking of his historic all-Black flight crew, greeting thousands of passengers flying coast to coast, and the many friends, Black and white, he made along the way.

He's flown so many miles on so many aircraft: the DC-6; DC-7; Lockheed Electra; BAC-111; Boeing 747, 727, and 767; Airbus 300; and more.

HE SMILES BROADLY WHILE THINKING OF HIS **HISTORIC** ALL-BLACK FLIGHT CREW ...

David likes to think back on his career and to consider what lies ahead. While he and Lyn have divorced since the events that took place in this book, they remain close: He plans to visit her and their daughter Leslie in Atlanta, Georgia, for Thanksgiving. He'll go see Cami and her family in Massachusetts for Christmas.

"Family is so important," he says. "Now, more than ever."

"Follow me back to the hangar," David says to a visitor.

Now 85 years old and having been retired from American Airlines for 26 years, he closes the cabin door on his airplane and speaks to his guest: "I would like to take one more flight in my Trinidad, my last flight," David says. He shows the visitor the flight instruments in the cockpit and explains the purpose for each knob and button. "But if I can't, I have many, many great memories in the air. I love flying. I always will."

David moves to sit on the wing of his airplane, one of his favorite perches these days, and takes a sip of cold water, contemplating the moment.

This Trinidad four-seat, single-engine airplane is David's last aircraft, a 3,000-pound reminder of his storied aviation career and, perhaps, his last days in the air piloting his own private airplane.

"Pretty soon I'll fix the plane to fly it, or I'll fix the plane to sell it. But I don't need to decide today," David says while staring into a cloudless blue sky. "But it sure is a beautiful day for flying."

AFTERWORD

Dr. Guion S. Bluford, Jr.
First African American in space

This is a story of an American hero. In this book, Michael Cottman describes the career of David Harris, America's first Black commercial airline pilot. Born in Columbus, Ohio, in 1934, David went to Ohio State University and got a degree in education. While there, he enrolled as a cadet in the Air Force Reserve Officer Training Corps (ROTC) and became interested in flying. This was at a time when few African Americans were pilots. None flew for commercial airlines, and those who wanted to, like the Tuskegee Airmen, who were hailed as heroes during World War II, were denied the opportunity. America was not ready to see African Americans in the cockpit. Despite frequent ridicule, harassment, and the lack of support by many, David worked hard and overcame those obstacles—all at a very volatile time in U.S. history. He earned his wings in the U.S. Air Force and became a commercial airline pilot for American Airlines. He flew thousands of hours for them in many different airplanes, including one of the world's largest, the Boeing 747. He excelled at what he did and became a captain, flying passengers all over the world.

My own story began some years after David's groundbreaking achievement; my career mirrors his. I grew up in the inner city of Philadelphia and became interested in airplanes. I wanted to be an aerospace engineer. After receiving a degree at Penn State, I joined the Air Force, became a fighter pilot, and fulfilled my dream of becoming an aerospace engineer. From there, I went on to earn my astronaut wings with NASA by flying four times in space, and eventually became a senior aerospace engineering executive. It's because of people who came before—people like David, who broke through racial barriers—that the path was opened up for others like me to follow in their footsteps.

How did David and I succeed? Through hard work, persistence, and determination. We both earned our college degrees and were able to ignore the naysayers and overcome obstacles along the way. We proved that African Americans can be commercial airline pilots, astronauts, or anything they want to be.

This is a story of David Harris and how he achieved his dream, and I hope this story inspires you to reach your dreams.

AFTERWORD

Lieutenant General Stayce Harris

✈

DEAR READERS,

If you've gotten to this point in the book, you already know how David Harris became the United States' first Black pilot for a major commercial airline. My name is Stayce Harris, and I am the second Black female pilot in the U.S. Air Force, now a retired lieutenant general living in Southern California. Although David and I share a last name, we aren't related by blood. Still, I'm honored to call him my friend and to share with you how our lives intertwined and, as a result, how he shaped who and where I am today.

It was 1985 and I was attending a convention for the Organization of Black Airline Pilots in Los Angeles, California. At 26, I was a brand-new C-141B transport pilot for the U.S. Air Force, and I was excited to meet other pilots of color who shared experiences of flying for commercial airlines and the military, like me. Back then, there were few Black pilots and even fewer Black commercial airline pilots. And you could count the number of Black female pilots on one hand.

David was at this convention, too, and was excited to see me: not only a Black female pilot but one that was currently serving in the Air Force as well. We hit it off, and that day was the beginning of what has become a lifelong friendship.

When I decided to make the career switch from the Air Force to becoming a commercial airline pilot, who was right there to offer words of wisdom and support? David Harris. In August of 1990, 26 years after David broke the barrier for Black people as pilots for commercial airlines, I was hired as a pilot for United Airlines. David couldn't have been prouder. I continued my service in the Air Force Reserve in February of 1991 and, in 2001, became the first Black female in the entire Air Force to command a flying squadron.

I stand on the strong, resilient, immensely qualified, and unapologetic shoulders of pioneers like my personal hero, Captain David Harris. It was an honor to serve our nation for 37 years, retiring as the Air Force inspector general and the first Black female to achieve the rank of lieutenant general in the Air Force. My career is a testament to the power of support, encouragement, and mentorship, and I'm proud to say I've adopted David's same passion for mentoring students who desire to follow in our footsteps and create exciting new paths of their own.

TIMELINE

Items above the timeline are from David Harris's life. Those below are key moments or events of historical or cultural significance.

1953 David enrolls in Ohio State University.

1956 David goes to ROTC summer camp at Tyndall Air Force Base in Panama City, Florida.

1957 David graduates from Ohio State University with a B.Sc. and an ROTC commission.

1958 David begins basic flight training at Bartow Air Force Base in Winter Haven, Florida.

1934 David Harris is born in Columbus, Ohio.

1930s	1940s	1950s

1939–1945
World War II

1947
Cold War begins.

1955 Emmett Till is murdered in Mississippi.

1955–1975
Vietnam War

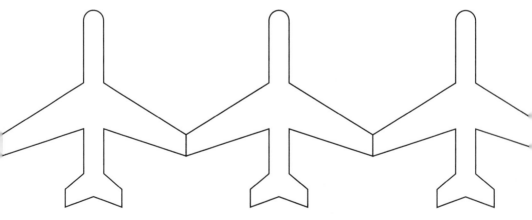

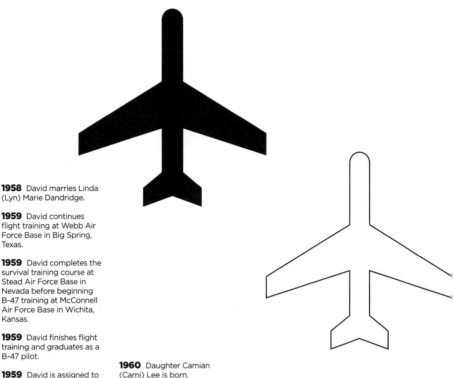

1958 David marries Linda (Lyn) Marie Dandridge.

1959 David continues flight training at Webb Air Force Base in Big Spring, Texas.

1959 David completes the survival training course at Stead Air Force Base in Nevada before beginning B-47 training at McConnell Air Force Base in Wichita, Kansas.

1959 David finishes flight training and graduates as a B-47 pilot.

1959 David is assigned to Plattsburgh Air Force Base in New York, as a B-47 co-pilot.

1960 Daughter Camian (Cami) Lee is born.

1963 Daughter Leslie Harris is born.

1960s

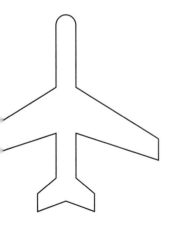

1962 Fannie Lou Hamer fought for the rights of thousands of African Americans to become registered voters.

1962 James Meredith is the first African American student to enroll at the University of Mississippi. Riots follow.

1962 Cuban Missile Crisis

1962 President John F. Kennedy signs an executive order banning segregation in federally funded housing.

1963 Joan Dorsey becomes the first African American flight attendant.

1963 Continental Airlines is ordered to hire Marlon Green in a landmark United States Supreme Court decision.

1963 March on Washington for Jobs and Freedom is held. Dr. Martin Luther King, Jr., gives "I Have a Dream" speech.

1963 Birmingham, Alabama, city schools are integrated by National Guardsmen under orders from President Kennedy.

TIMELINE

Items above the timeline are from David Harris's life. Those below are key moments or events of historical or cultural significance.

✈

1964 David is granted permission to leave the U.S. Air Force.

1964 David is hired by American Airlines as the first African American pilot for a major passenger airline.

1965 David and his family move to the Boston suburbs.

1967 David is made captain with American Airlines.

1971 David flies the American Airlines charter flight for Whitney Young's funeral.

✈ **1960s** **1970s**

1963 16th Street Baptist Church bombing in Birmingham kills four young girls. In response, James Bevel and Diane Nash begin the Alabama Project, which will later grow into the Selma voting rights movement.

1963 President Kennedy is assassinated.

1964 Three civil rights workers, James Chaney, Michael Schwerner, and Andrew Goodman, disappear and are later found murdered.

1964 President Lyndon B. Johnson signs the historic Civil Rights Act.

1964 Dr. King is awarded the Nobel Peace Prize.

1965 Alabama State Troopers attack unarmed marchers on Selma's Edmund Pettus Bridge in an event known as Bloody Sunday.

1965 Dr. King leads a march from Roxbury to Boston Common in Massachusetts to protest school segregation.

1968 Dr. King is shot and killed in Memphis, Tennessee. Riots break out in more than 150 U.S. cities in response to the assassination.

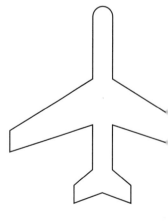

2018 David is honored by a Tuskegee Airmen memorial group in his hometown of Columbus, Ohio.

1984 David arranges American Airlines' first all-Black flight crew.

1994 David retires from American Airlines.

2019 David is honored by Sisters of the Skies.

1980s　　　　**1990s**　　　　**2000s**

1991
Cold War ends.

2008 Barack Obama becomes the first African American president elected to the United States.

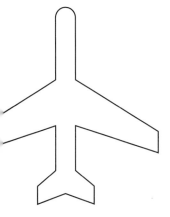

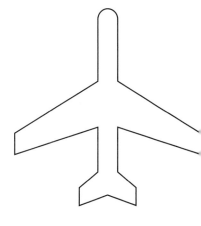

AUTHOR'S NOTE

✈

I was only eight years old when David was hired by American Airlines, in 1964, as the first African American pilot flying for a major commercial airline.

In 2017, I was in Atlanta visiting my aunt. While there, I decided to look up the widow of my mentor, the celebrated writer Lee May.

That woman was the accomplished journalist Lyn May. As I sat in her comfortable living room, we spoke about the colorful Japanese maples, rose bushes, and hydrangeas that adorn her garden. Then we turned the conversation to books about notable African Americans and, eventually, David Harris, Lyn's ex-husband.

"You should really meet David," Lyn said. She went on to tell me fascinating stories about David's life. I knew that his career had progressed as the civil rights movement unfolded. I'd come to see that through his unique, individual story I could look deeper into the struggle that African Americans endured during this time in history.

I called David the next day, and we talked nonstop for two hours. He told me all about his challenges while training to become a pilot in the military and with American Airlines. He reflected on his brilliant and rewarding career. I knew there would be many complicated and complex layers to his narrative. His words captured me, and I had to know more.

David invited me to meet with him at his home in a rural airpark community in South Carolina. One trip was not enough. I visited David several times. He showed me photos that spanned his career in aviation, and we talked at length about his friends and heroes, whose photos hung on the walls. With each visit, David beamed with pride while sharing story after story about his thrilling high-flying days as a pilot. Enthralled, I knew I wanted to write a book about his experiences.

I took copious notes and digital recordings during my nearly two years interviewing David. It's an honor to share David's journey, the story of a man I admire and respect. I hope young readers everywhere will also be inspired by David's tales of overcoming adversity to become someone extraordinary.

ACKNOWLEDGMENTS

Segregated Skies is dedicated to David Harris for his tenacity, perseverance, and commitment to rise above racism during turbulent racial times in America. David was a pioneer who broke barriers to become the first African American pilot to be hired by a major commercial airline, a landmark development in 1964, even as President Lyndon B. Johnson signed the historic Civil Rights Act. Thank you, David, for allowing me to share your phenomenal journey.

Segregated Skies is also dedicated to Lyn May, David's former wife and a good friend of David's to this day, a formidable woman who kept David focused on his quest to become an Air Force pilot and then a successful commercial pilot. Lyn was David's confidant, adviser, and sounding board when David needed to privately vent about his racist run-ins. Lyn and David were partners who battled, survived, and succeeded together.

Thanks to Lyn for being David's touchstone and for urging me to write this book. Lyn's intellectual vision and editing skills are extraordinary. Thank you, Lyn, for sharing your amazing personal story of perseverance and courage with me— and with the young readers who will turn these pages and be inspired by the many teachable moments from your shared experience.

And thanks to Lee May, my mentor, friend, and father figure who is watching over us and guiding us from above.

To my parents, Howard and Roberta Cottman, thank you for showing me how to soar.

To my superb and talented literary agent, Jenny Herrera: I appreciate your guidance and encouragement throughout this entire project.

A special thanks to David's daughters, Camian and Leslie, who embraced me like family and shared their extraordinary personal stories about their aviator father, who, along with Lyn, instilled in them a sense of adventure, family values, and integrity.

Thanks to my lovely daughter, Ariane, for offering continued encouragement the past 18 months while I was conceptualizing, writing, and researching, and while you are teaching our next generation of kids. I love you dearly.

Thanks to Yolanda Woodlee and Keith Jones for their steadfast support, friendship, and, once again, opening their beautiful home for me to write this book in peace, beauty, and solitude on the banks of the Chesapeake Bay.

And a heartfelt thank you to Dr. Alison LaVigne, whose steadfast reassurance, advice, and love helped me complete this project. Thank you for listening on so many occasions when I read these pages aloud and offering valuable feedback even after you returned home from a long day at the office treating cancer patients. I appreciate you today, tomorrow, and for the many days to follow.

Thanks also to Rene LaVigne, Jr., for his helpful transcription services—much of it under constant deadline pressure—and for his professionalism, our conversations about the Black experience in America, and his good-natured approach during the entire book-writing process.

To my wonderful family, Pat, Carol, and Rod: Thank you for opening your homes and your hearts to me so often. From Atlanta to Sacramento, you have helped shape my life in ways I could never imagine. You have helped me become a better father, friend, and nephew. I couldn't do life without you—and I wouldn't want to try.

I am thankful to have two of the best editors in the industry: Ariane Szu-Tu and Erica Green. Ariane and Erica brought a deep sense of compassion, intellect, and a profound understanding of culture that helped shape the pages of this book. I've worked with many editors throughout my 35-year career as a journalist and author, and few possess the sensitivity to edit a complex story about race and aviation. I am grateful to these extraordinary editors. Thank you, Ariane and Erica, for offering me the platform—and the intellectual freedom—to share David's powerful story with young readers across the country and around the world.

The publisher would also like to thank the book team: designer James Hiscott, Jr., photo director Lori Epstein, fact-checker Jennifer Geddes, and production editor Joan Gossett, as well as Graciano Petersen for his sensitivity review, Stephanie Hartsfield and Sisters of the Skies for their Foreword contribution, and Stayce Harris for her Afterword contribution.

FURTHER READING

10 True Tales: Young Civil Rights Heroes, by Allan Zullo, Scholastic, 2014.

Aircraft: The Definitive Visual History, by DK, 2013.

Flight: Discover the Remarkable Machines That Made Possible Man's Quest to Conquer the Skies, by DK Eyewitness Books, 2011.

Freedom Riders: John Lewis and Jim Zwerg on the Front Lines of the Civil Rights Movement, by Ann Bausum, National Geographic, 2005.

Freedom Walkers: The Story of the Montgomery Bus Boycott, by Russell Freedman, Holiday House, 2009.

Marching to the Mountaintop: How Poverty, Labor Fights, and Civil Rights Set the Stage for Martin Luther King, Jr.'s Final Hours, by Ann Bausum, National Geographic, 2012.

Students on Strike: Jim Crow, Civil Rights, Brown, and Me, by John A. Stokes, National Geographic, 2007.

Who Were the Tuskegee Airmen?, by Sherri L. Smith, Penguin Workshop, 2018.

CREDITS

All personal photos and memorabilia courtesy of David Harris. Photo of David Harris with plane by Travis Dove. Special thanks to Travis Dove for photographing Mr. Harris and his collection of photos and keepsakes.

COVER: (UP and back cover, clouds), RUNSTUDIO/Photodisc/Getty Images; author photo, courtesy of the author; 2-3, RUNSTUDIO/Photodisc/Getty Images

INDEX